D0050110

# An Atheist

# Defends Religion

### Bruce Sheiman

ALPHA

A member of Penguin Group (USA) Inc.

*This book would not have been possible without the continued love and support of my fiancée Sherrie Casali and my mother and father.*

**ALPHA BOOKS**

Published by the Penguin Group

Penguin Group (USA) Inc., 375 Hudson Street, New York, New York 10014, USA

Penguin Group (Canada), 90 Eglinton Avenue East, Suite 700, Toronto, Ontario M4P 2Y3, Canada (a division of Pearson Penguin Canada Inc.)

Penguin Books Ltd., 80 Strand, London WC2R 0RL, England

Penguin Ireland, 25 St. Stephen's Green, Dublin 2, Ireland (a division of Penguin Books Ltd.)

Penguin Group (Australia), 250 Camberwell Road, Camberwell, Victoria 3124, Australia (a division of Pearson Australia Group Pty. Ltd.)

Penguin Books India Pvt. Ltd., 11 Community Centre, Panchsheel Park, New Delhi—110 017, India

Penguin Group (NZ), 67 Apollo Drive, Rosedale, North Shore, Auckland 1311, New Zealand (a division of Pearson New Zealand Ltd.)

Penguin Books (South Africa) (Pty.) Ltd., 24 Sturdee Avenue, Rosebank, Johannesburg 2196, South Africa

Penguin Books Ltd., Registered Offices: 80 Strand, London WC2R 0RL, England

**Copyright © 2009 by Bruce Sheiman**

All rights reserved. No part of this book shall be reproduced, stored in a retrieval system, or transmitted by any means, electronic, mechanical, photocopying, recording, or otherwise, without written permission from the publisher. No patent liability is assumed with respect to the use of the information contained herein. Although every precaution has been taken in the preparation of this book, the publisher and author assume no responsibility for errors or omissions. Neither is any liability assumed for damages resulting from the use of information contained herein. For information, address Alpha Books, 800 East 96th Street, Indianapolis, IN 46240.

International Standard Book Number: 978-1-59257-854-2
Library of Congress Catalog Card Number: 2008943862

11   10   09      8   7   6   5   4   3   2   1

Interpretation of the printing code: The rightmost number of the first series of numbers is the year of the book's printing; the rightmost number of the second series of numbers is the number of the book's printing. For example, a printing code of 09-1 shows that the first printing occurred in 2009.

*Printed in the United States of America*

**Note:** This publication contains the opinions and ideas of its author. It is intended to provide helpful and informative material on the subject matter covered. It is sold with the understanding that the author and publisher are not engaged in rendering professional services in the book. If the reader requires personal assistance or advice, a competent professional should be consulted.

The author and publisher specifically disclaim any responsibility for any liability, loss, or risk, personal or otherwise, which is incurred as a consequence, directly or indirectly, of the use and application of any of the contents of this book.

**Trademarks:** All terms mentioned in this book that are known to be or are suspected of being trademarks or service marks have been appropriately capitalized. Alpha Books and Penguin Group (USA) Inc. cannot attest to the accuracy of this information. Use of a term in this book should not be regarded as affecting the validity of any trademark or service mark.

Most Alpha books are available at special quantity discounts for bulk purchases for sales promotions, premiums, fund-raising, or educational use. Special books, or book excerpts, can also be created to fit specific needs.

For details, write: Special Markets, Alpha Books, 375 Hudson Street, New York, NY 10014.

# Contents

# Introduction:
# The Great Debate Stalemate

The theism-atheism debate has been dominated for centuries by two positions: Hard-core believers fervently committed to the argument that there is a personal God who created the world and offers humans salvation; and militant atheists vehemently driven to repudiate not only God but also religion as a cultural institution. As if to accentuate and reinforce this polarity, we have had a plethora of recent books presenting atheists' tried-and-true position *there's no proof for God* and theists' predictable counterclaim *there's no proof that there's no proof.*

I have found that when religious apologists strive to demonstrate the existence of a divine creator in light of what science reveals about the natural world, they engage in rationalizations that are unfathomable to an unbeliever. And atheists express their side of the debate by resorting to a polemical subterfuge, using science to claim that God does not exist. (Science, as I will explain, is actually silent about the existence of God.)

In neither case is the rationale very convincing to the other side. What neither theists nor atheists are prepared to admit is that after more than 2,000 years of back-and-forth proofs and counterproofs, this debate has reached an insolvable impasse.

## Going Beyond the God Question

The time has come to reach beyond the God question and accept that it can never be resolved to the satisfaction of either side. But the discussion need not end there. We are still left with the important issue of the *value* of religion itself. And this is a debate that religion can win.

*An Atheist Defends Religion* is a robust response to the numerous recent books by unbelievers—with a twist. I am an atheist. But unlike most atheists who embrace their rejection of God as a sign of intellectual triumphalism, I assert that such disbelief is maladaptive and that some form of theism is the overwhelmingly preferable option. *An Atheist Defends Religion* defines a unique middle position in the theism-atheism controversy that affirms the *belief in* God without getting mired in the interminable debate about the *existence of God*. And I must emphasize, this is a first. To date, there has not been a mainstream book defending religion as a cultural institution, irrespective of the God question.

*An Atheist Defends Religion* is not for the dogmatic minority on either side of the God debate. It is intended for the "moderate majority" of religious America: people who are not militant atheists or literalist believers; people who accept that science *and* religion are essential for a fulfilling life.

## Defending Religion, Not God

In this book I provide a more thoughtful interpretation of the theism-atheism debate than has hitherto been offered. I am not affiliated with any religious doctrine or partisan perspective. Consequently, this book is not dominated by one extremist view or the other.

I must disclose that I am not a person of faith: I do not feel the majesty or mystery of God. But neither do I stridently repudiate God. Indeed, there is a part of me that *wants* to believe in God. That makes me an *aspiring theist*. And I want to believe in God because, on balance, religion provides a combination of psychological, emotional, moral, communal, existential, and even physical-health benefits that no other institution can replicate.

This book, as a consequence, is not a defense of God; rather, it is a defense of the belief in God, and of religious belief in general. And this book will not respond to atheism with a list of tried-and-true "proofs" of God's existence. Rather, it will persuasively show that atheism is an impoverished belief system, and that, individually and collectively, we are much better off with religion than without it.

It is very much like the distinction William James made in *The Varieties of Religious Experience* between a "healthy-minded" and a "sick soul" temperament. Both personalities, curiously, live in the same world. But in the former, optimism and openness prevail; people essentially see the world as loving and inspiring. In the latter, pessimism and despair predominate; people largely see the world as tragic and hopeless.

For most people this dichotomy refers to the very real difference between religious belief and the antibelief of atheism.

## My Personal Journey to Ambivalence

My own spiritual and intellectual journey has been circuitous, but increasingly I find myself on a path that brings together belief and unbelief. I grew up in a religious-neutral, theologically confused household. My mother was marginally Christian and my father was barely Jewish. I went to a Jesuit college and learned to do what Jesuits do— question everything, including religion. Self-reflection and critical reasoning were the forces that molded me into an obstinate atheist.

Critical reasoning is our educational system's most cherished practice. But it has a dark side. At first it leads to relativism, based on the assumption that all cultural truths are equally valid. In time, critical reasoning takes us a step further, to the view that all beliefs are equally dubious, equally subject to skepticism. And so it was with my already faint religious orientation.

For me, the core idea of religion is belief in a Transcendent Spiritual Reality that exists apart from the material world we experience day-to-day. In accepting that my here-and-now existence is all there is, in either Western or Eastern traditions, I qualify as an unbeliever. Unlike other atheists, however, I have never resorted to the reverse psychology of making my unbelief into a virtue.

Being an atheist is not something that I rationally or deliberately chose. I did not think through all the competing belief systems and choose unbelief. It's just something that *I am*. I must admit, however, that the more I understand the world as revealed by science, the more I find the materialist and reductionist explanation for our human destiny terribly devoid of depth, value, and meaning. This offends not my religious sensibility (of which I have none), but my *existential vanity*—the strongly held personal view that *my life counts* in the scheme of things. As a consequence, I am an atheist who is sympathetic to religious aspirations and who is prepared, if not to defend God (in no place in my book do I assert that God exists), then to defend the belief in God.

## Red Pill and Blue Pill

No work of popular culture better depicts the world envisioned by atheists than the movie *The Matrix*. In it, the character Morpheus says to our hero, Neo, "The Matrix [read: *religion*] is the world that has been pulled over your eyes to blind you from the truth." It is a "prison for your mind." When pressing Neo to take the Red Pill that will reveal the full extent of the Matrix's deceit, as opposed to the Blue Pill that will perpetuate the delusion, Morpheus says, "All I'm offering is the truth, nothing more."

After more than half a lifetime, I have learned that there is a difference between lowercase truth (facts and knowledge) and uppercase Truth (wisdom and fulfillment). I did not know it at the time, but I took the Red Pill. The "truth" may set us free—but I have also learned that freedom is just an empty vessel that must be filled with something spiritually meaningful. I now wish that I had taken the Blue Pill.

As an aspiring theist, I want to believe that our universal spiritual longing for wholeness and perfection is suggestive of the divine. I want to believe that the reason we finite beings reach out to an ineffable and unfathomable Absolute is because we are *Imago Dei*. I want to believe that our timeless quest for goodness and transcendence has its Omega Point in God.

I want to believe this—but, alas, I cannot. Thus, even though I cannot believe in God, I still feel the need for God.

## The Significance of Religion

A mature view holds that religion is more about meaning and purpose than facts and events. Through religion, we experience the mundane as miraculous and the normal as numinous. Religion teaches us that our lives have inherent worth and that the world is shot-through with value. Paul Tillich said, "He who enters the sphere of faith enters the sanctuary of life." And that is because the core preoccupation of religion is the preservation and perpetuation of human existence. The question I present here is not whether God exists (in my mind, he does not), but whether the world is a better place because people believe God exists. More than any other institution, religion deserves our appreciation and respect because it has persistently encouraged people to care deeply—for the self, for neighbors, for humanity, and for the natural world—and to strive for the highest ideals humans are able to envision. And there is no more eminent ideal than religion's clear declaration of human specialness and the absolute sanctity of life. This book reflects the perspective of anthropologist Robert Torrence: "Religion is no luxuriant excrescence upon the trunk of society, but a fundamental expression of underlying values that society can articulate in no more effective form."

## The Economics of Theistic Belief

I approach religion much like an economist. I believe religion persists in our market-based culture, despite the prevalence of secularism, because it provides net value over and above its required investment, and because it beats competing belief systems in the same value proposition. Belief systems, whatever their purported veracity, rise and fall by the benefits they provide and costs they incur to individuals, groups, and society. I evaluate religion in terms of its pragmatic usefulness to humankind and seek to answer the question posed by William James: "Grant an idea or belief to be true, what concrete difference will its being true make in anyone's actual life?"

Thinking about religion in broad economic terms is not far-fetched. It is well documented that a major reason for America's religiosity is that our country is the world's first free market for religion. The competition fostered in a free-market environment motivates theological organizations to offer religious consumers innovations that translate into higher levels of participation. In America, orthodoxy is minimal and choice is maximal. Such consumer segmentation and product differentiation makes for a very "efficient" religious marketplace. None of this disparages religion; indeed, these dynamics have made America the most religious nation in the developed world.

Atheism, as I will show, is a bankrupt ideology on empirical grounds: Its benefits simply do not come close to covering its opportunity costs. Religion, on the other hand, offers the vast majority of people a high-value transaction: Its enduring benefits far outweigh its costs. Religion persists, in short, for the reason that it provides the greatest good for the greatest number of people.

The economics of theistic belief are best capsulized in this variation of what is known as Pascal's Wager: If we wager that God does not exist and he does, then we have everything to lose and nothing to gain. If we wager that God does exist and he does (or even if he does not), then we have everything to win and nothing to lose *in this life*.

Indeed, the biggest of religion's alleged liabilities—wars and violence—are not fully a function of religion, but result from the *politicization* of religion. Much of religion's perceived negative effects derive from the same influences that corrupt all institutions. Thus, much to the chagrin of unbelievers, sectarian violence would not appreciably diminish with the elimination of theistic belief. This book examines what is intrinsic to religion *qua* religion—absent the distortion caused by political interference.

Incidentally, the notion that people cannot think rationally or think for themselves, or that they are beguiled by their own ignorance or deceived by malevolent religious potentates—these are all cynical excuses put forth by atheists to explain something they find deeply incomprehensible: Why believers do not repudiate religion and accept reason as their savior just as they do. It is simply because religion provides substantial net-positive benefits that no other institution can come close to matching.

## The Affirmative Dimensions of Religion

Thousands of books have addressed the question, "What is religion?" My paradigm makes a distinction between what *consumers* of religion experience (meaning, values, purpose) and what *producers* of religion offer (organization, doctrine, scripture). By emphasizing believer experience rather than institutional offerings, we obviate the need to justify any particular religious tradition. Instead, we can focus on what I have identified as the *affirmative dimensions* that make up religious experience. In other words, in the economic value equation, religion offers believers several distinct but integrated benefits that reflect actual psychological, social, emotional, moral, and existential rewards.

Human beings everywhere think about the nature of reality and the right way to live, and many are led from those questions to speculate about the divine. Because religion deals with such ultimate concerns, its influence trickles down into every facet of human existence and conduct. Therefore, to understand human experience, it is necessary to understand religion. As the theologian Robert Kress has written: "When we study religion, we study how the *whole* of human existence is lived and explained."

*An Atheist Defends Religion* is the first book to identify and evaluate the affirmative dimensions of the human spirit that find expression in religion. What explains the persistence and pervasiveness of religion is a confluence of irreducible positive factors that cannot in total be replicated by any other institution. Taken together, they powerfully explain why religion is so enthralling, enriching, enlightening, empowering, and enrapturing. They explain how it is that we achieve our fullest humanity only in religion.

# Life, Liberty, and the Pursuit of Religion

The debate about the existence of God is neverending. What is not in dispute is that God exists in people's hearts, minds, and spirits. What is not in dispute is that religion is adaptive, constructive, and healthful—and thereby makes a positive difference in people's lives. Reflecting James's pragmatic conception of belief: When we act as if religion is true, we act with greater optimism, hope, and benevolence.

Faith is one of the most powerful forces in human development and a strong impetus to personal transformation and collective progress. In addition to purely individual expressions and experiences, this book will also discuss the religious foundations of and contributions to science, human rights, democracy, social reform, technology—indeed, all of civilization.

The take-away from this book is that religious experience is the essential human experience. The hopeful path of human history—its renaissance, reformation, and enlightenment—would not have been possible without religion. Mine is a human-centric evaluation of religion. By any empirical measure—defined in terms of theism's practical impact on individuals, society, and culture—religion is profoundly beneficial.

In the end, this book will cogently explain that the most rational and definitive argument for dismissing atheism is not to be found in the interminable debate over the existence of God, but rather in demonstrating and elucidating the enduring contributions of religion. Religion's misdeeds may make for provocative history, but the everyday good works of billions of people is the real history of religion, one that parallels the growth and prosperity of humankind. There are countless examples of individuals lifting themselves out of personal misery through faith. In the lives of these individuals, God is not a delusion, God is not a spell that must be broken—God is indeed great.

Daniel Dennett, one of the most vociferous atheists, has written that "I'm so optimistic that I expect to live to see the evaporation of the powerful mystique of religion." But I submit that the affirmative dimensions of religion described herein are important reasons such "evaporation" is not conceivable. And Dennett is missing another key feature of modern religion that ensures it will continue to flourish: religion's ability under free-market conditions to grow, adapt, evolve, and mature.

Militant atheists like Dennett assume that religion is static, but religion is as dynamic as the societies in which it is found. The fact is that religion is not a primitive artifact of some prescientific age. It is very much a modern institution that continues to serve people's deepest needs.

## Humans Are Driven by Absolute Value

I will come back to this theme again and again. More than anything, human existence is about value; specifically, I propose that the ideal of *absolute value* is at the heart of human experience. I will explain later where this need for supreme value comes from, but suffice to say that humankind takes the basic formulations of biological value—what promotes life is "good" and what negates life is "bad"—to the highest level of cultural abstraction. The major thrust of this book is that humans do not just seek the evolutionary imperatives of a full stomach and ample mating partners. Because of our acute awareness of insurmountable physical and temporal limitations, because we see ourselves as the embodiment of all that is impermanent and insignificant in the universe—we seek absolute worthiness, which has its highest expression in religion.

What is noteworthy about religion is that it uniquely embodies our highest expressions of value. And that makes all religions—Eastern and Western, modern and ancient—to borrow a phrase from Rudolf Otto, "outwardly diverse but inwardly akin." From this conception of value flow the three central dimensions of religious experience:

- **Connection with Creation:** Through myth and ritual, humans achieve a cosmic meaningfulness and participate in the sacred drama of the universe (Chapter 1).

- **Devotion to Humanity:** Through morality and altruism, people achieve supreme goodness and a oneness with all mankind (Chapter 2).

- **Union with the Divine:** Through salvation and transcendence, humans achieve the highest of all ideals, Absolute Value (Chapter 3).

The actualization of these three religious dimensions in turn results in mental health and fulfillment (Chapter 4) and, over time, offers humanity its best prospects for the growth and progress of civilization (Chapter 5).

As the word implies, religion is about relationships: our relationship to God, to humanity, and to the world. In all instances, the nature of that relationship is love and devotion. From our loving relationship with the highest value (God), we experience a heightened sense of our own intrinsic worth, which permeates our relations with other people and the universe. Thus religion in its most profound simplicity is about our relationship to the highest values we are able to envision.

## Am I Really an Atheist?

This question comes up time and again. How can an atheist defend religion? As I hope will become clear in these pages, I defend religion as a *cultural institution*, just as I might defend the global capitalist system or the value of science to humanity. I call myself an "aspiring theist"— I admit that I sincerely want to believe in a personal God, in the soul and the afterlife. Life is a miraculous creation. But I do not believe that my life was created by a Supreme Spiritual Being and I do not believe that my life force survives my death.

For the majority of the world, human *dignity* is predicated on human *divinity*. I do not personally believe that. But there's something in me that wants to. And at a minimum, if I cannot embrace the existence of God (no matter how hard I try), I can have regard for the belief in God. In my view, it is no longer only an issue of the veracity of religion, but an issue of the *value* of religion itself.

For more commentary, readers are invited to visit AnAtheistDefendsReligion.com, and you can direct your feedback to Bruce@AnAtheistDefendsReligion.com. I look forward to receiving your insights and comments.

# Religion Is Finding Life's Meaning: Myth, Ritual, and the Sacred

What is the meaning of *meaning?* For most people, as the cliché goes, it is the connection to something larger than ourselves—finding purpose in a framework that is broader than our daily lives. I think this definition is generally correct, but in need of a little refinement. In my understanding, we experience meaning when we are able to place our lives in an existential framework that links us to the three transcendent dimensions that encompass our individual lives—humanity, nature, and the universe. And I am not referring to just any universe, but a universe that overflows with *value*.

## The Religious Worldview

All spiritual questions pertain to our place in the universe; we all seek a world of infinite value that envelopes and embraces us. And when we frame humanity's primordial question like that, we come to realize that no theoretical system is more effective in conferring ontological value than the religious paradigm. No belief system comes closer to granting us transcendent meaning than the religious worldview, which tells us that not only do we live in a universe of supreme value, but the source of that universe loves and exalts us. It is no wonder that every search for meaning is a search for the sacred.

The primary impetus behind religion, therefore, is the endeavor to live a sanctified life, a life of heightened value—psychologically, existentially, and morally. Value pervades every aspect of the religious person's world. To be sure, all nonreligious people also seek lives pervaded by value. The difference between the religious person and the secular is that devout Christians, Muslims, Jews, and Hindus are able to derive the values of their lives from the highest source that humans can conceive: the transcendently good, eternal, and omnipotent.

Religion originates in the uniquely human awareness of the isolated *self* standing naked in a world of enormous power and vast potentiality. Other animals have a purely utilitarian relationship with the outside world. Only humans understand that this world exists apart from the needs of the self: an infinitesimal being surrounded by infinity. The moment we become aware of this larger world, we desire a meaningful relationship with that world, which for thousands of years has been best mediated by religion.

One of the most insightful observers of religion was the late Mircea Eliade, who understood the core of religion to be a relationship with the sacred:

> *Whatever the historical context in which he is placed,* homo religious *always believes that there is an absolute reality, the sacred, which transcends this world but manifests itself in this world, thereby sanctifying it and making it real. He further believes that life has a sacred origin and that human existence realizes all of its potential as it participates in the sacred.*

## Primitive Societies as Homo Religious

In this chapter, I spend considerable effort addressing the experience of primitive societies, which I consider to be exemplary of religious experience in general. It is not my intention to disparage modern religion by using primitive culture to help understand the religious mindset. I am focusing on early human society for two reasons. First, primitive man is religious man par excellence; he is *homo religious*. As contemporary Westerners, we are correct to think the primitive person is inferior from a purely secular perspective (in the context of science, technology, politics, and social organization). That is exactly why he makes such a good model for understanding religious behavior: he is completely religious and not at all secular. But from the standpoint of brain chemistry and function, modern and primitive people are the same.

Another reason for my selective emphasis on early human culture is because primitive man was so *honest* about his ambitions. If we took a survey of modern people, we would need to cut through so much secular clutter and verbiage that we may never be able to understand humanity's true motives. Studying early societies reveals explicitly how humans, more than anything, want to participate in a world suffused with the highest symbolic value. And I believe that any observer who can see through the static and noise of our pluralistic and variegated society would see clearly that we moderns seek the same thing as primitive man: to immerse ourselves in high-value cultural contexts.

As I previously stated, perhaps the most distinctive characteristic of archaic culture is the lack of a secular life apart from religious life. Unlike modern societies where even the most pious and devout spend a substantial part of their lives outside of a religious milieu, the primitive's life was pervaded with religious ritual, myth, and symbolism. In modern culture, the experience of the sacred is removed from day-to-day activity. But to archaic people it is self-evident, accessible, and more real than the material world. The genius of primitive society, in its religious coherence and purity, is that to the ordinary man *nothing is ordinary*. For a religious man, nature is never only "natural"; it is always fraught with religious import. And this was so easy for the religious person to grasp because the entire cosmos was believed to be a divine creation.

The primitive's life was imbued with ultimate meaning because he was following a script prepared and sanctified by the primordial gods. This is far different from modern times when a person is in the presence of divinity only when he is in a church, synagogue, temple, or mosque. In contrast, the primitive man was *always* in the presence of the gods. According to Eliade, "The man of archaic societies tends to live as much as possible *in* the sacred or in close proximity to consecrated objects. For primitives the sacred is equivalent to power and, in the last analysis, to *reality*. The sacred is saturated with *being*."

## Everything Is Sacred

Here is an interesting example showing how everything in the primitive world was permeated with the sacred. According to the cultural anthropologist A. M. Hocart, even something as secular as money, specifically gold coins, had a religious origin. In ancient Indian Vedic mythology, gold was believed to be the seed of Agni, the fire god. And gold was also seen as partaking in the nature of the sun and was substituted for the sun in ritual. In an Indian ritual in which a gold plate is made, the ritualist says: "For this gold plate is the same as truth. Yonder sun is the same as truth. It is made of gold: for gold is light and the sun is light; gold is immortality, and he is immortality; it is round, for he is round. Indeed, this gold plate is the sun."

According to Hocart, this passage suggests a common origin for the gold coin, the king's crown, and the halo, all three being representations of the sun's disc; it also explains the circular form of our coinage.

Religion further explains why sovereign heads of state or monarchs appear on coins: kings for centuries were understood as representatives of the divine on Earth.

Thus for religious man, the entire world is suffused with the sacred—spirits and gods that brought the world to life. The monotheism of Judaism, Christianity, and Islam reflects the realization within human consciousness that all of reality is a unified whole, that behind the diverse expressions of power, mystery, and majesty is an underlying holiness.

A feeling of profound connection binding humans with the rest of creation characterizes the convictions of most religions. Humans see behind the cycles of life—birth and death, growth and decay, hunger and satiation, despair and joy, sleep and wakefulness—a broader spiritual world of meaning and purpose. The Unitarian Universalist minister Galen Guengerich had this to say: "Religion unites the purpose of our lives as human beings with the purpose that animates the universe. Religion unites the meaning of our lives as human beings with the meaning that pervades the universe. Religion unites the spirit of humanity with the spirit that keeps the stars shining, the planets spinning, and the flowers blooming."

The perceived order and harmony in nature is the archetypal spiritual experience. It is the first reason that comes to mind when people are asked to explain why they believe in God. After what began in early society as the unseen power of animism—other words to describe the sacred have included *wakanda* (Souix), *orenda* (Iroquois), *mulungu* (Bantu), and the Latin *numen*—emerged pantheism, from which was derived polytheism and finally monotheism, the idea that behind the universe resides a single Transcendent Spiritual Reality.

## Man Exists on Two Planes: Sacred and Profane

Perhaps the most pervasive religious understanding of the human condition is that man exists on two levels simultaneously: sacred and profane, earthly and heavenly, material and spiritual, the realm of animals and the realm of gods. Man's life, says Eliade, "is lived on a twofold plane; it takes its course as human existence and, at the same time, shares in a transhuman life, that of the cosmos or gods." This is a universal conception of human duality that is found in all cultures. Humanity is at the center of a cosmic drama that takes place on two planes of existence. What is essential to understand is that these two planes are distinguished by their *valuation:* one is positive (good, powerful, eternal) and the other negative (evil, mortal, sinful). Through myths and rituals, man is able to bridge the two realms. Thus in *The City of God,* St. Augustine stated that during our time on Earth the Christian inhabits two worlds—the earthly and the heavenly—and at the end of time God will integrate the two into a single kingdom.

Anthropologist Ernest Becker described the primitive religious practices of *macrocosmization* and *microcosmization*. In the former, man takes the elements of his mundane life and extends them to the realm of the gods; in the latter, man humanizes the cosmos by bringing the celestial down to the corporeal world. In this way, man and the eternal are intertwined. For ancient man, everything on Earth had a celestial counterpart, a heavenly parallel. He imitated the acts of the gods: "Thus the gods did; thus men do." Temples were constructed "in accordance with the writing of the sky." A lucid example of this intermingling of the celestial and the terrestrial in man is provided by the Babylonian mode of time-reckoning as reported by Hugo Winckler and cited in Otto Rank's *Art and Artist:*

> In the Babylonian mathematical tables the number
> 12,960,000 is treated over and over again .... The sig-
> nificance of this number has been explained to us by Plato
> .... According to him, this number was the arithmetical ex-
> pression for the law controlling the universe .... The year,

> reckoned at 360 days, makes 12,960,000 days = 36,000
> years. And this, according to Babylonian calculation, is the
> number of years in a world-age. Plato reckons the duration
> of a human life at one-hundred years (= 36,000 days), so
> that one day of a man's life corresponds to one year of the
> universe world-year. Thus the two numbers of man and the
> universe (and therewith the godhead) are brought into an
> inward relation: they are mirror-images of one another.

Myths and rituals have many pragmatic purposes for social organization and the regulation of individual behavior. But to focus only on those functions, which is easy for a secular Westerner to do, is to miss the essential point of these religious practices: they help man to sanctify every aspect of his life. These heaven-earth homologies bring together the finite with the limitless, the mortal with the eternal, and the material with the spiritual.

## Myth and Ritual Are Complementary

Humans have always had a deep-seated need to feel that what they are doing is supremely meaningful in the broad scheme of the universe. Each person wants to feel an intimate connection to and integral role in the workings of the world. And it is through religious myths and rituals that man is placed firmly at the center of things.

When we analyze the myriad religious myths and rituals of the ages, in every case what they seem to be doing is make man into a "hero"—a vital and active participant in the cosmic drama of the gods. Each culture, according to Becker, "is a mythical hero-system in which people serve to earn a feeling of primary value, of cosmic specialness, of ultimate usefulness to creation, of unshakable meaning." All religious activity is thus "supernatural" in the sense that it is aimed at raising man above nature—above the limitations of a physical, temporal existence.

Through religious myth and ritual, man's purpose is bound up with the higher purpose of the universe.

There are hundreds of books about myths and about rituals, as if they were separate and distinct cultural phenomena. But they are actually two sides of one religious experience. Myths impart knowledge about the realm of the gods, and rituals enable humans to participate in this divine dimension of reality. Both are part of one essential religious experience that confers higher purpose and truth. As Hocart said, "Thus the myth is part of the ritual, and the ritual part of the myth. The myth describes the ritual, and the ritual enacts the myth." Myth is a script for ritual performance in which the participants actualize the meaning of life. And this was a world in which archaic man participated, not every Sabbath, but all day and every day. Through myth and ritual, the world is made comprehensible and infinitely significant.

## Myth: Explaining the World

Myths today are universally understood as fictional narratives with allegorical messages. Our modern views of mythology have been colored by interpretations of early Greek myths as a form of literature. Accordingly, for most people mythology is considered an early effort at recording history, offering mere metaphorical explanations of how things got to be the way they are.

The anthropologist A. M. Hocart also recognized that modern understandings have debased the meaning of mythology:

> In the course of their explorations, the scholars of the Renaissance came upon Sophocles and Eschylus, but they interpreted the drama of those times as they interpreted their own stage—as literature enacted. They failed to realize that the early Greek drama, literary as it might be, was still something more than mere theatricals, and that the myths

*were enacted not merely to amuse, but because the religion demanded it.*

We must understand that when myth becomes little more than a Greek tragedy presenting "morals" and "lessons" to an audience of spectators, it is no longer a myth in the most meaningful sense. A myth can be said to be *alive* only when the person is fully engaged in the myth— that is, as a *participant*. The power of myth dies the moment we become spectators. For most people today, myth is a vernacular expression that connotes "unreal" or "fictional." Thus, once we label something a myth, any religious meaning is *dead*. This is unfortunate because myths actually form the most important part of religious tradition. As we will see, the only "live" myths are those that are truly lived.

Another misconception about myths is perpetuated by observers who suggest that myths are to be found *everywhere*. To these writers, a "myth" is any cultural or personal construct—which is to say, all beliefs, archetypes, dreams, stories, symbols, literature, and memories. Writing in *Parallel Myths*, J. F. Bierlein offered this over-generalization: "Myth has something to say to everyone, as it has something to say about everyone: it is everywhere and we need only recognize it." And I found this definition in Karen Armstrong's *A Short History of Myth*: "Myths are universal and timeless stories that reflect and shape our lives—they explore our desires, our fears, our longings, and provide narratives that remind us what it means to be human."

For these observers the study of myth has become a vast and encompassing discipline—indeed, after the success of Joseph Campbell, mythology has become a veritable industry. And therein lies the problem: If myth can be anything to anybody, it ultimately has no meaning, which is ironic because myths are about nothing but meaning. Thus, my understanding of myth is somewhat less ambitious and more clearly defined than the aforementioned.

I am referring to Eliade's understanding of myth—which is to say, in a purely religious sense. A *living* myth depicts man's participation in the divine realm wherein one's daily life flows with transcendent meaning. Through myth and ritual, archaic man relived the epics of the gods and heroes; he participated in eternal life and gained control of the mundane world. In the days of the living myth, there were no atheists; there was no secular world of any kind. Man was unable to speak of anything beyond the world as given by the gods. Myths delineated reality as a single, meaningful, and inclusive whole from which all particular aspects of the world are derived.

Myths reveal our connection to the divine world as well as our role and destiny within that larger world. And it is not enough to know the myths of origins and heroes—one must also recite them, reenact them, and *live* them. He who recites or performs the origin myths is thereby steeped in the sacred atmosphere in which these miraculous events took place. By "living" the myths, one emerges from profane, chronological time and enters a time that is of a different ontological quality, a "sacred" time. Myths are intended not just to explain the natural world, but also our special place in the world. It elevates humans to the level of gods and gives man a starring role in the cosmic drama.

A myth is true not because it is factual, but because it is *meaningful*. But that suggests an interesting paradox about myth: Today when we call something a "myth," we mean that it is somehow less real than our empirical experience. In religious culture, a myth depicted that which is *more* real than our mundane existence. And all myths are *religious*—having to do with ultimate concerns, with the sacred mode of existence.

This is crucial to understanding myth. By this definition, there are no secular myths because all myths are about the Transcendent Spiritual Reality and are thus religious. Sacred history is considered true because it conveys the original acts of creation by the supernatural beings. Because myth relates the actions of transcendent beings and the manifestation of their sacred powers, it lays the foundation for all human behavior and all social and cultural institutions. Eliade again: "Myth narrates events that took place in primordial Time. Myth tells us how, through the deeds of Supernatural Beings, a reality came into existence. Myth, then, is always an account of a 'creation'; it relates how something was produced, began to *be*."

The principal myth is the *creation* myth, which in religious tradition expresses an understanding of the ultimate meaning of the world and of human existence. The purpose of creation stories is to connect this life with its divine origin; understand how our lives became estranged from that divine origin; and reveal how to achieve salvation through a reunion with the divine source. Thus the creation myth explains more than just the beginning of the world, but also why we are mortal, why we are subject to suffering and tribulation, why evil and imperfection exist, and the role of moral conduct in realizing the ultimate reunion with the divine.

The truth myths express pertains to the existential question of how to live fully meaningful lives. The function of religious creation stories is not primarily to explain events in the distant past, but to locate present human experience in a larger framework of significance.

## Ritual: Life's Passages and Progressions

It is important to understand that in religious societies, every person was an active participant in the cosmic drama. And it is easy for us to forget the religious function of rituals when our own rituals have become purely secular and, to use Eliade's term, "desacralized." For the religious person, rituals are techniques for enhancing and elevating life to the highest level of worthiness. It is through ritual that archaic man reaffirmed contact with the world of the gods and participated in their creative works.

Throughout history, rituals have been used to accommodate and facilitate the growth and maturation of each member of society, whose life was structured as a series of progressive stages mediated by rites of initiation. Eliade said that initiation rituals "in the most general sense denote a body of rites and oral teachings whose purpose is to produce a decisive alteration in the religious and social status of the person to be initiated." Rites of passage make the cycles of birth, adolescence, marriage, childbearing, aging, and death meaningful by putting them on a plane of spiritual significance. Anthropologist Paul Radin understood this: "Birth, puberty and death were very early recognized as an unending cycle, in which an individual passed from one level of existence to another."

For primitives, life was not a curve as we see it in secular terms, where birth is zero and death is return to zero. For religious man birth was zero, and at each successive stage one draws value from the divine realm, where death is considered the final promotion of a soul to infinity. Death is only death to the profane condition of man, followed by rebirth into the sacred realm of eternity. In so doing, man intertwines his destiny with that of the immortals.

It was Eliade who recognized that initiation ceremonies corresponded to the creation myth: "On the occasion of each rite of passage, man takes up again from the beginning the world's drama: the repetition of the cosmogony." Rites of initiation are in every case a rite of metaphorical death and renewal or rebirth, just as the cosmos was created out of chaos. Ritual death signifies a temporary return to chaos; it is the paradigmatic expression of the end of one mode of being and the beginning of another.

Initiatory death signifies at once the end of childhood, of ignorance, and of the profane condition. As Eliade said, "Initiatory death is indispensable for the beginning of spiritual life. Its function must be understood in relation to what it prepares: birth to a higher mode of being." In philosophical terms, initiation is equivalent to a basic change in existential condition; the novice emerges from his ordeal endowed with a totally different being from that which he possessed before his initiation.

From one religion to another, from one wisdom tradition to another, the significance of rites of passage and their corresponding myths is the continual reaffirmation of man as participating in the cosmic drama and graduating to higher states of existence. We see this in Christian initiations: baptism (cleansing of the soul; forgiveness of sins; a renewed life), communion (a union with Christ), and confirmation (reaffirmed commitment to Christ). Even in Buddhist rites of passage this symbolism is retained. The Buddha taught the way of dying to the profane human condition—ignorance and suffering—and being reborn to the freedom and bliss of Nirvana.

## Myths, Rituals, and Modern Man

Secularists today, of course, will say: It's all well and good that myths and rituals provide religious people with a feeling of transcendent purpose—but it's based on *untruth*; it's all factually incorrect. Secularists will also say that modern man does not live in mythic religious time, but in real historical time, where death is anything but a graduation to a higher state of being. As a secularist myself, I am compelled to agree with that. But I must admit it amounts to a true loss of meaning.

### Secularism's Loss

Religious myths and rituals previously integrated all dimensions of life and elevated that life to the highest status by subsuming it under a divine purpose. The modern world, however, is characterized by a fragmentation of roles, experiences, and cultural contexts. For most people, there exists a tension between the religious and secular worlds. And for many others, there is only a secular world with no religiosity allowed. I tell myself that the devaluation of myths to fictional stories and rituals to secular holidays is the price we pay for a freer, more pluralistic culture. But in the process of modernization, secular people have certainly lost something significant: *We no longer feel like we belong to the universe*.

The secularization of man did not go unnoticed by Eliade. Decades ago he made an explicit distinction between those of us who live in "historical time" (of the temporal world) and the ancients who lived in "sacred time" (of the eternal world). "Modern man's originality, his newness in comparison with traditional societies," wrote Eliade, "lies precisely in his determination to regard himself as a purely historical being, in his wish to live in a basically desacralized cosmos."

The idea that religion offers a profound sense of purpose is unfamiliar to many of us. As I have said, all myths and rituals have religious origins. When desacralized, however, they become vestiges of their former relevance. According to Eliade, "Desacralization pervades the entire experience of the non-religious man of modern societies and, as a consequence, he finds it increasingly difficult to rediscover the existential dimensions of religious man."

There is a need to create secular versions of religious meaning. But the question for me is whether that will ever be entirely possible. My conclusion after decades of studying the human condition from every perspective—psychology, philosophy, theology, and anthropology—is that there may not be much in the secular world alone to compensate for or replace religious meaning.

Myths and rituals were the vehicles that placed humans in the realm of the sacred. Archaic and traditional societies invented myth and ritual to transcend the mundane world. Yet the secular version of the "sacred" is deficient. In our culture, even the most religious among us spend most of our time in the secular realm. As secular people, we lack overarching explanations for the forces that govern our lives. Our trials, tribulations, tragedies, and transitions lack a larger purposeful context. People in traditional societies, which by definition were religious societies, encountered few existential mysteries that did not have an answer that included humankind as a central participant. But for secular man the transcendent meaning of the cosmos as conferred by the religious framework has been lost.

By developing a secular culture apart from religious culture—in economics, politics, business, education, and recreation—we have been able to create a modern world of our own, a world of prosperity and freedom that would never have been possible in an absolutist religious context. So to a large extent, the secular divergence from religious society has been highly worthwhile. Yet what we end up with are mainly secular remnants of religious myths and rituals that may help to root us in our communities, but not much more. None of them can provide the sense of overarching meaning and purpose that religious conceptions once did. In Eliade's terms, the mundane or secular is the "profane" dimension of existence and we have little "sacred" to turn to for elevation or inspiration.

## Can Science Replace Religious Myth?

Science has proposed a creation story of its own. And the great advantage of this story, atheists like Richard Dawkins will tell us, is that it is matter-of-fact *true*. No need for fiction or falsity. Furthermore, the scientific creation story is thoroughly awesome and fascinating.

A truncated version of the scientific creation theory goes like this. Almost 14 billion years ago, the big bang created the universe of space and time from a "singularity" the size of a mathematical point; within the first second of this explosion, the nascent universe expanded faster than the speed of light in a phenomenon known as cosmic inflation. The big bang created matter and antimatter particles; they obliterated each other, except for a small excess of matter that allowed our universe to take shape. But that small excess is *a lot* of stuff: just 4 percent of the current universe accounts for all the ordinary matter that we can see through our telescopes (accounting for hundreds of billions of galaxies each containing hundreds of billions of stars), with 22 percent of the matter in the universe being of the "dark" variety (invisible and unknown at this time), and the remaining 74 percent of the universe consisting of "dark" energy (an unknown repulsive force counter to gravity that is making the universe expand at an accelerating rate). According to one of many long-term scenarios, in 100 billion years or so all matter will be so widely distributed that an observer within one galaxy in the universe will not be able to "see" any galaxy anywhere else in the universe; in other words, our destiny is the ultimate in cosmic loneliness.

What becomes apparent is that the scientific creation story is in conflict with a literal interpretation of the religious creation story. And despite the persistence of many unknowns, I have no doubt that the scientific conception is correct. My concern, however, is less about the incompatibility between scientific theory and religious myths, and more that the scientific version of the Alpha-and-Omega story is so lacking in personal meaning.

Scientists who are not religious say they are able to derive a spiritual sense of meaning from this scenario, which is usually some vague reference to the wonder and beauty of creation as revealed by science. But for the majority of people this is an unconvincing argument. While most of us can readily understand the concept of gravity, for example, we cannot so easily comprehend phenomena on the micro-level of particle physics or the macro-level of cosmology. The big bang, dark matter and energy, cosmic inflation, antimatter, black holes, weak and strong forces, and the Higgs boson are not easily comprehensible to the layperson. Even staunch atheists cannot tell you they really understand what these scientific variables mean; they merely accept them as revealed truth (even if it requires a humongous particle accelerator and esoteric mathematics to prove it).

We must recognize that we are all inclined to believe what appears most accessible to the human mind. The beauty and complexity of the universe seems to suggest a divine creator. This appears plausible, if factually incorrect. But I have to look at what science gives to us—a universe that is far too complex for my feeble mind.

As an atheist, I accept what science says about the universe, but it unfortunately does not convey any meaning for my life. The physicist Steven Weinberg was correct when he stated, "Science has weakened people's view of God. The universe used to be much more mysterious, but now we know more." It is true that we know more, but we understand less, from which we derive even less meaning.

Science is the best tool we have for forging reliable knowledge about how the world works. But *how* the world works is not *why* the world works. The world of myth offers more meaning than mere descriptions of natural laws. No one can deny the success of science; it works because it is true. But in our drive to discover lowercase truth (facts and knowledge), we have sacrificed uppercase Truth (meaning and purpose), which was provided by religious myths and rituals. Thus, according to science, our place in the universe is negligible. We have the distinction of being a monad standing discrete and alone in a sea of infinity.

After the Enlightenment, humans were awash with utopian visions of reason, science, and technological advancement as a replacement for religious strivings. During this period, the significance of religious myth diminished, but not the human need for meaning and purpose. For a time, many secularists were able to derive meaning from feeling that they stood at the forefront of scientific knowledge and technological progression. That lasted until the latter part of the twentieth century, when we saw an explosion of New Age religions replacing the secular visions of progress, which themselves had replaced the religious myths of old. Of course, for most of us, New Age religions are flakey and insubstantial, which is why more recently we have witnessed a renaissance of traditional religion in an attempt by many people to return to their spiritual origins.

But many more of us have been left behind to grapple with the existential predicament I call the Modernist Paradox: *Religion does not satisfy me because I do not believe it is true; science is true, but it lacks substantive meaning.* In the same context, Karen Armstrong has written, "Myth had made human beings believe that they were bound up with the essence of the universe"; yet in a world dominated by science we are told that humans occupy "only a peripheral place on an undistinguished planet revolving around a minor star." The world as revealed by science is a summation of impersonal laws and mechanistic forces. Thus we can be forgiven for yearning for a religious world that is thoroughly suffused with the sacred and is fully alive to humanity.

The difference between the scientific worldview and the religious worldview is the difference between humans having an "I-It" relationship with nature and an "I-Thou" relationship. Humans cannot tolerate a silent world, a world that does not acknowledge our existence. We want to live in a loving universe. Thus God becomes the Universal Thou. In the religious worldview, everything in this world is endowed with life, so that every phenomenon appears as a "Thou" in the sense that Martin Buber used this term. We need the world to recognize and acknowledge us. This is more than a need for other people. We yearn to feel enveloped by a *universal sentience*. We want to encounter not an "It" but another consciousness, a "Thou." In fact, this is the most meaningful definition of the sacred—as the Universal Thou that permeates the cosmos, lies behind the world, and infuses the world with purpose and value.

In the religious scenario, the world is said to be *alive* for the believer. That is why the believer can say that *everything* is proof for the existence of God. The world is eminently responsive to the believer who has a personal relationship with God.

## The Inadequacy of Secular Rituals

Not only are secularists without religious myths offering a central purpose for humanity in the universe, we also have few meaningful rituals. Vestiges of the "new world" rituals can be found in modern initiation ceremonies and in such cyclical cultural phenomena as New Year celebrations, but not much else.

I can offer a few observations about where modern secularists have been able to derive a modicum of transcendent worthiness. As one salient example, watch what happens when a person is in the presence of a secular "god" or "goddess" (celebrity). Or note the exhilaration we feel when we embrace any "sacred" consumable object (women: shoes; men: cars). We might laugh at this phenomenon, and certainly not all people seek satisfaction from such shallow endeavors, but what is clear is that in the secular world, as in the religious, we ache to be a part of a high-valuation context. Fame, wealth, celebrity, power, physical beauty: these are the social values many of us seek that enable us to participate on the level of the secular sacred.

The archetypal ritual, as previously discussed, is the initiation rite of passage that correlates with the cosmogony and manifests as a symbolic death-rebirth experience. It is fascinating to look at areas in our secular culture where the death-rebirth experience is expressed. In a prosperous society, rarely do we confront actual death. As a result, many people actively contrive scenarios where death looms prominently in the background.

I have always been more than a little curious of people who, under the guise of "recreation," voluntarily expose themselves to overt danger. In the name of "excitement," more and more people in prosperous Western societies are risking their lives to the point where activities like extreme sports have become an industry of some scale. The goal is not only to manifest maximum exertion, but to explicitly court extinction and come out alive. Steve Fossett, an adventurer who was the first person to fly nonstop around the world in a balloon, no doubt felt godlike one summer morning when he took out his private plane without any survival gear, and was never heard from again. It's exhilarating to tempt death and emerge alive, but are we really that bored in a world without the religiously sacred? Of course, there have always been people who risked their lives merely for the thrill of it, but it is a statement that so many people today willingly and eagerly engage in activities the final outcome of which weighs heavily against survival. It seems that when we are brought to the brink of death and we survive, this is the greatest death-rebirth experience we can possibly have outside of a Bimin-Kuskusmin (Papua New Guinea) initiation ceremony.

The great majority of us, of course, do not knowingly put our physical lives at risk. Available to us are numerous cultural and symbolic opportunities for death-rebirth experiences. Watching a sporting event, for example, enables us to experience the imminence of death (defeat) and the exhilaration of rebirth (victory). Even something as simple as a suspenseful movie has the protagonist facing impending death and the triumph of good over evil as an exhilarating rebirth. In both sports and business, when the home teams win we become heroes, vanquishing the enemy and celebrating victory. It was George Allen, the famous football coach, who said it nicely: "The winner is the only individual who is truly alive …. Every time you win, you're reborn; when you lose, you die a little."

This is similar to the symbolic death and rebirth cycles that are enacted in primitive rituals. The difference is that rarely are these contemporary rituals suffused with divine value; they are secular rather than religious. When we were able to experience rituals in a religious context, they acquired a cosmic significance that was infinitely more satisfying than what is provided in our modern culture.

When we come to realize that myths and rituals, in the mind of the religious person, are not mere fallacies or coping mechanisms but a reflection of a higher reality, we can only come to understand much of our modern secular world as a huge comedown. In our secular rituals, we are not participating in a cosmic event that was performed at the beginning of time by supernatural agents; rather, often we are repeating a mundane event that offers little more than a mini-experience of personal renewal. I do not mean to suggest that most secular endeavors are lacking depth or substance. Certainly many secular people live highly productive and meaningful lives. But we must also recognize that secular activities do not elevate us to a higher state of being where we commune with the universe's eternal powers, but serve generally to give us a momentary sense of personal uplift.

The religious mindset of intertwining human and cosmic forces, of making man godlike, may seem like quite an admission of grandiosity; but that cosmic heroism, as Becker put it, is what a thoroughly religious person experiences every day, as he is forever immersed in the divine reality. Consider the qualitative difference between the religious and secular worldview: the secularist may feel fortunate to have tickets to a sold-out Broadway performance; that, however, is negligible compared to being a potent participant in the cosmic drama of the world's creation and redemption.

Secularists may console themselves with the notion that they are living firmly in reality and not in a fantasy world; and they may condescend toward this "primitive" thinking for its scientific implausibility. But it is a great tragedy that modern science does not give humans even a tiny supporting role in the cosmic drama. As I have said elsewhere, lowercase truth (the facts of science) is important, but it is purely utilitarian; it enables me to start my car in the morning and watch television news in the evening. But that is not uppercase Truth, which provides a deep and fulfilling sense of my integral place in the universe I call home.

# Religion Is Caring for Humanity: Community, Morality, and Altruism

An integral part of religion pertains to morality: how we interact with our fellow human beings and, increasingly, with all of nature. In this chapter, I will answer two questions: "Does religion make people good?" and "Can people be moral without religion?" Even though these questions appear to be contradictory, my answer to both is a resounding *yes*. However, there needs to be a number of qualifications.

Our moral nature grows directly out of our social nature. Social anthropologists attribute the development of human morality to group harmony. But humans exhibit ethical behavior that goes well beyond the explanatory power of group cohesiveness, and that is precisely where religion comes into play.

## Religion Is Community

William James famously defined religion as consisting of "the feelings, acts, and experiences of individual men in their solitude, so far as they apprehend themselves to stand in relation to whatever they may consider the divine." As much as I admire James, in this case he is decidedly incorrect. Religion is not an individual matter; it is foremost a communal affair.

Rather than James, a more informed understanding of religion comes from the father of sociology, Emile Durkheim, who was specifically interested in religion as a communal experience: "Religion is eminently social. Religious representations are collective representations which express collective realities." And this makes sense. The word "religion" is derived from the Latin verb *religare*, which means "to tie together; to bind fast." The original meaning of religion pertained to binding oneself to God. Later the term would also be used to designate a bonded belief system and set of practices. But its meaning pertaining to the binding of people together under a common faith logically follows.

Empirical research reveals that religious activity is associated with greater social cohesiveness. In one of many studies working with survey data, researchers examined the relationship between religious involvement and social ties in a sample of 3,000 households in the southeastern United States. The results showed a positive relationship between religious involvement and both the number and quality of social connections. The average person who attends church several times a week enjoys 2.25 times more nonkin ties than the person who never attends. Another study by anthropologist Richard Sosis drew on a catalogue of nineteenth-century communes published in 1988. He chose 200 for his analysis, 88 of which were religious and 112 secular. Sosis found that communes whose ideology was secular in nature were up to four times as likely as religious ones to dissolve in any given year.

If religion is the original community-building institution, then it stands to reason that it also is a preeminent morality-building institution, because social organization always implies standards of behavior. And while that is certainly true, religion ultimately does much more. It is also largely responsible for civilization's most important moral accomplishment: a universal humanist ethic.

## Religion Is Morality

When we review the fundamental tenets of the major religions, we find they have in common a strong moralistic orientation. Moral values are central to a religious view that claims the world was created by a loving, all-powerful God concerned with human flourishing, and that posits a supreme goodness as the basis for all reality. The fundamental moral position that flows from a religious conception is that all of life, being a mode and manifestation of that ultimate reality, is holy and intrinsically valuable, and that moral action is the path to a union with God. This understanding necessarily obligates the believer into a moral contract under which by doing good he is participating in the highest good, the natural outcome of which is overflowing compassion and a deep, intuitive certainty of the common linkage among all living beings.

The fact that all religions attempt to explain the prevalence of evil in the world suggests further that the foundation of their beliefs is goodness—goodness in the deity and goodness in humankind. Thus intrinsic to all religions is a moral imperative. This cannot be said of any other cultural institution. Because God created all things, all things deserve to be revered, and by living in conformity with God's commands humans achieve as close an identity with God as can be had in this life. The equation of religion with absolute goodness is total. If the basis of sin (or, in the case of Eastern religion, the ego-illusion) is that man has separated himself from the divine source, it makes eminent sense that the way to a reunion with the divine is through the renunciation of sin and the perpetuation of good works. The way to Heaven or Nirvana, the liberation of the soul or atman, is through actions that conform to God's goodness.

Atheists often exhibit a lack of understanding of religious morality. They assume that, for the believer, morality is very simple: whatever

God dictates is right is right, and whatever God dictates is wrong is wrong. Atheists speak about religious morality purely as a reward-and-punishment relationship to mythic parental figures. Religious people are seen as moral automatons; believers are commanded to *obey*. The most cynical see in religion a blind obedience to moral authority and an oppressive behavioral-control system.

There is no question that some religious adherents exhibit an authoritarian orientation, but the same can be said for many nonreligious people. (I have encountered more than a few sanctimonious atheists.) For the vast majority of people, however, authoritarianism is not the defining feature of religious morality. God is not seen as a parent in a disciplinary or authoritarian sense, but in the sense of a loving father who teaches the way to achieve salvation or liberation. God represents the moral high ground to which humans aspire.

The great moral advancement of religion comes from putting forth an ethical code that is rooted in an Absolute. God is understood as eternal, omnipotent, omniscient, and infinitely good. That is not a coincidence: When we conceive of Absolute Value, goodness is an integral and inherent part of that conception. Thus, participating in the world of an infinitely loving God always implies a moral relationship between man and God and, by extension, man and man.

Every major religion stresses the objective existence of moral ideals, the importance of moral conduct, and the possibility of individuals and societies attaining a good and happy life. The believer sees a God who holds humans to the highest moral standards; and he feels a loving obligation to do what is right for God and for other human beings. Religious people do not strive to be good because they want to avoid punishment and earn bonus points in the heavenly sweepstakes; they strive to behave consistent with God's love and grace in much the same way we naturally strive to be good for anyone we love.

The most essential contribution of religion to cultural values is the sense of the sacred, of something so absolutely good that it is worthy of unconditional reverence. As with rituals and myths, morality is another manifestation of humans identifying with the highest values. And it is through good works that humans participate in these values. Righteous deeds, charitable acts, service to others, and ethical adherence are all primary vehicles for reaching heavenly redemption.

And this is true in Eastern as well as Western conceptions. The Supreme Self of many Indian religions is a reality of great wisdom and bliss, knowledge of which leads people to see all things as part of the Divine Self and worthy of reverence, union with which can be attained by leading lives of compassion and good works. The Tao of Heaven in East Asian religions is a basic moral order written into the structure of the universe, calling people to live in accordance with that order of justice and laying down ways of life that will bring fulfillment and inner happiness.

Humans were said to be made in the image of God, an ideal that laid the ground for a Christian humanism that made individual persons objects of respect in their own right. Since humans were meant to share in the divine nature, they are to be respected as children of God and not treated as a means to an end. So wrote St. Augustine in his *City of God:* "Whoever is born anywhere as a human being, that is, as a rational mortal creature, however strange he may appear to our senses in bodily form or color or motion or utterance, or in any faculty, part or quality of his nature whatsoever, let no true believer have any doubt that such an individual is descended from the one man who was first created."

Such a moral conception has led to the highest sacrifices among humans. Albert Schweitzer's deep religious conviction led him to renounce prestige and comfort to go to Africa and provide medical care for thousands. Martin Luther King's dream of a society in which all people would live freely together was essentially a religious vision. Religious conviction lay behind Mahatma Gandhi's life of asceticism and nonviolent protest. And for literally millions of less-celebrated people, their countless acts of sacrifice and compassion every day help to uplift humanity's condition.

If religion does motivate some people to perfidy, it is more than balanced by the myriad good deeds performed in the name of God every day. It is unfortunate that a large conflagration attributed to religion attracts far more attention than the billions of small candles lit by religious people all over the world.

According to Giving USA, American charitable contributions reached a total of $307 billion in 2007, a figure that represents more than 2 percent of GDP, well above that of any other nation in the world. Of that $307 billion, 33 percent was given to religious organizations— or just over $100 billion. And of that, an undetermined amount went to further the charitable mission of thousands of religious initiatives, from feeding the poor to international relief efforts. As just one example that takes place literally hundreds of times every week: Addressing a conference of 6,000 Methodist youths in North Carolina in 2007, a bishop made an appeal for $10 donations for mosquito nets to save African children from malaria. Within minutes, they had raised $14,000. What other force has the power to raise so much money so quickly to help people on a distant continent?

Sociological studies forcefully argue that religious beliefs are correlated with moral behavior. Research cited by Rodney Start and William Sims Bainbridge showed that moderate religious people are more caring and compassionate than their nonreligious peers, and give more money to charity. Sociologist Arthur Brooks, who has performed extensive research on charitable giving, has shown that religious people are 38 percent more likely than secularists to give money to charity and 52 percent more likely than nonreligious people to volunteer their time. Thus in 2000, religious people donated about 3.5 times more money per year ($2,210 versus $642) and volunteered more than twice as often (12 times versus 5.8 times). Indeed, when looking at the difference between the populations that give the most versus the least, on a percentage-of-income basis, religion is the most salient predictor.

Looking at other measures of religious affiliation, people who pray every day (whether or not they go to church) are 30 percentage points more likely to give money to charity than people who never pray (83 percent to 53 percent). Further, people who say they devote a "great deal of effort" to their spiritual lives are nearly twice as likely to give as those devoting "no effort" (88 percent to 46 percent). Moreover, these practices are not exclusive to particular religions. It does not matter what religion one practices so long as it is practiced seriously. Among those who attended worship services regularly in 2000, fully 92 percent of Protestants gave to charity, compared to 91 percent of Catholics, 91 percent of Jews, and 89 percent of other religions.

Arthur Brooks is the leading expert in America about the demographics and characteristics of charitable giving, having evaluated the results of dozens of studies and authored the book, *Who Really Cares*. Although the charity gap is not as great when we examine giving to nonreligious causes, religious people were still 10 percentage points more likely than secularists to give to nonreligious charities such as the United Way (71 percent to 61 percent) and 21 points more likely to volunteer for secular causes such as the local PTA (60 percent to 39 percent). In addition, the value of the average religious household's donations to nonreligious charities was 14 percent higher than the average secular household's. The same is true when it comes to informal acts of kindness to others. Religious people were far more likely to donate blood than secularists, to give food or money to the homeless, and to express empathy for less fortunate people. In yet another example of religious charity, about 1.6 million U.S. churchgoers travel on short-term mission trips each year, devoting their time and money to build schools, deliver medical aid, or feed orphans.

By doing what God prescribes, one is accepted by God and participates in the realm of the divine. Doing good means being good, and within the divine context that means attaining the highest value; one's life is validated on the highest level. Thus believers do not do what is right because they think God wants them to, but because they feel it serves the ultimate purpose of God.

It is clear that the idea of moral and spiritual progress is at the very center of religion. And an evaluation of religious truths reveals a fundamental consensus on moral principles. Biblical scholar Lewis Browne illustrated the shared morality of the world's great religions with these variations of the Golden Rule:

- Brahmanism: "This is the sum of duty: Do naught unto others which would cause you pain if done to you." (*Mahabharata* 5, 1517)

- Buddhism: "Hurt not others in ways that you yourself would find hurtful." (*Udana-Varga* 5, 18)

- Confucianism: "Is there one maxim which ought to be acted upon throughout one's life? Surely it is the maxim of loving-kindness: Do unto others what you would have them do unto you." (*Analects* 15, 23)

- Taoism: "Regard your neighbor's gain as your own gain, and your neighbor's loss as your own loss." (*T'ai Shang Kan Ying P'ien*)

- Zoroastrianism: "That nature alone is good which refrains from doing unto another whatsoever is not good for itself." (*Dadistan-i-dinik* 94, 5)
- Judaism: "What is hateful to you do not to your fellow man. That is the entire Law." (*Talmud, Shabbat* 31a)
- Christianity: "All things whatsoever ye would that men should do to you, do ye even so to them: for this is the Law of the Prophets." (*Matthew* 7, 12)
- Islam: "No one of you is a believer until he desires for his brother that which he desires for himself." (*Sunnah*)

The central idea of this book is that what is most sought in every human endeavor is Absolute Value, and what we seek to avoid is *relativism*. Humans cannot live in a world where ethics are relative. Thus, while it is true that without religion people can certainly have a morality, it is problematic if that morality is not felt to be rooted in something objective and absolute. The paradox is that the moment we think that our moral precepts are man made, we immediately feel they are fallible and insubstantial. No one wants to believe that their value system is culturally or historically arbitrary. Few people are comfortable believing their value system is a function of personal opinions, individual preferences, or calculating self-interest (even if it often is).

We all have a strong need to feel that what we believe in—from the facts of the universe to the principles of morality—is anchored in objective truth. That is what we need above all else, to feel that what is right is rooted in an absolute good that transcends human will. And there is no higher source of truth than a divine being from which all creation emerged. Religion thus becomes the most important cultural and institutional source of ethical principles precisely because it is felt to be above human caprice.

## Our Innate Moral Sensibility

As a secularist, I must admit that I do not really believe that our morality comes from God. So the question remains: If not God, where then does morality come from? Harvard psychologist Marc Hauser thinks he has the answer: Morality originates from an innate sense of right and wrong. In this understanding, morality evolved like any other intrinsic capacity—for the good of the individual and society.

According to Hauser, "We evolved a moral instinct, a capacity that naturally grows within each child, designed to generate rapid judgments about what is morally right or wrong based on an unconscious grammar of action." He found that moral decisions are made intuitively, rather than consciously or rationally, and that people come up with similar answers when faced with particular moral dilemmas regardless of culture, religion, and income. "Moral judgments," Hauser wrote in his book *Moral Minds*, "are mediated by an unconscious process, a hidden moral grammar that evaluates the causes and consequences of our own and others' actions."

Hauser measured people's morality by using hypothetical scenarios that usually begin like this: "A runaway trolley is about to run over five people walking on the tracks …" or "You pass by a small child drowning in a shallow pond and you are the only one around …." These "tests" have been given to thousands of people around the world, and the very interesting result is that all people responded much the same way. Further, he has shown that atheists respond in a manner almost identical to religious people.

This finding usually leads to a "eureka" response from secular humanists like Hauser, who believe this proves that religious people are no more moral than atheists and agnostics. He concludes from his research that "across a suite of moral dilemmas and testing situations,

Jews, Catholics, Protestants, Sikhs, Muslims, atheists, and agnostics deliver the same judgments." Hauser has also written that "our own nature, not God, is the source of our species morality." And he further states, "These observations suggest that the system that unconsciously generates moral judgments is immune to religious doctrine."

It is clear that Hauser's aim is to prove that there is no difference in morality between religious and nonreligious people. And on the level of innate moral faculty, I think he is correct. But Hauser's work suffers from one huge deficiency: Nowhere in his 400-page book does he seriously pay attention to the factors that result in the gap between moral instinct and actual behavior.

Being an academic, Hauser seems unconcerned with *real* human moral behavior. Thus Hauser neglects the most important question to arise from his book: If we all intrinsically know what's right and good, why don't we all behave that way? There is a need for an *intermediate* dimension between the innate sense of right and wrong and the actualization of moral behavior. And in this, religion plays an indispensable role.

In truth, our innate moral capacity is really just a vague moral inclination that points us all in the same direction. And I think it is nebulous for a reason: It accommodates different situations and some amount of free choice. But that also means there is no guarantee that any situation will in fact result in the most moral actions. I am not here suggesting, like Jean-Jacques Rousseau, that we are born to be good and society corrupts us. Rather, I believe science shows us that we are born with an undercurrent of good that is ready for adaptation, but which must first be activated, articulated, and actualized through *culture*. This moral sense is not so strong that it dictates instinctive behavior, but it is not so weak that it is easily corrupted. In fact, for the vast majority of us in the vast majority of circumstances, it serves us well. This is to say that people are innately good, but such goodness remains largely a *potentiality* and does not mean that people will always do the right thing. For that, contrary to the cynical perspective of Rousseau, we *need* culture.

It makes sense that the evolution of our nervous system would be biased in favor of pro-social behavior for the sake of our collective survival. But what Hauser completely neglects to explain is why if we are hard-wired for moral behavior we can be so *immoral*. Our history is one long list of people doing the wrong thing thinking that it is the right thing to do. Thus being in possession of a moral instinct does not mean that people will always do the right thing. In reality, there is a huge gap between our innate moral tendencies and our actual behavior. That gap is bridged by culture. And because of the almost infinite variability of culture, it is consequently a long and variegated path to actual moral behavior, which is where religion comes into play. Therefore to say that people do not need religion for moral guidance is incorrect.

## The Moral Behavior Paradigm

Hauser's conceptualization does not begin to articulate the complexity of moral decision-making. I suggest that our moral behavior results from a complicated interplay of eight factors on five interrelated levels, wherein religion plays an essential role both historically and currently. The following five levels begin with two universal dimensions, one intrinsic (moral sensibility) and the other externally given (religious principles); followed by two cultural dimensions, one applying to all people in a society (laws, education) and the other pertaining specifically to the individual's immediate environment (parenting, peer groups); finally, these dimensions are influenced by an individual's distinctive genetic makeup.

34

Level 1—Intrinsic Universal: Innate Moral Sensibility

Level 2—Extrinsic Universal: Religious Moral Principles

Level 3—Extrinsic Objective: Social Contract, Education, Laws

Level 4—Extrinsic Subjective: Parenting, Peer Group Norms

Level 5—Intrinsic Subjective: Genes

The interrelationships among these five levels are so variable that it is almost impossible to generalize. The two absolute pillars are the Intrinsic Universal (innate moral sense) and Extrinsic Universal (religion). Over time, these absolutes are filtered through the level of Extrinsic Objective, which codifies the moral absolutes into broad social norms, institutionalized education, and laws. On a more immediate level, these norms and principles are further filtered through the level of Extrinsic Subjective where they can split and diversify like light through a prism.

## Level 1—Intrinsic Universal: Innate Moral Sensibility

As already noted, we are born with an inherent moral sensibility. But I think it is a pure potentiality that requires tremendous acculturation over time. At the core of this moral playbook is the unconditional principle that we acknowledge every individual as a person who deserves to be treated as we want to be treated—essentially a combination of Kant's second formulation of the Categorical Imperative ("If I use a person as a thing, I myself lose my dignity as a person") and the Golden Rule. But, again, this intuitive orientation must be articulated, objectified, and codified if it is to influence actual behavior.

## Level 2—Extrinsic Universal: Religious Moral Principles

Religion has been the foremost articulator and explicator of these inchoate moral precepts. Remarkably, with respect to generalized situations, religions agree much more than they disagree. And this is because, I believe, they are the primordial linkage with the universal innate capacity.

Religion deserves its own category because it is antecedent and pervasive, because it trickles down to all other levels, and because it is attributed to an absolute (divine) source of validation. The greatness of this moral principle is that it accepts and tolerates all people, including those who we might otherwise find unacceptable. My enemy is united with me in something that is above him and above me, the ultimate ground of being that is in each of us (the absolute good).

Interestingly, this moral capacity is rarely felt as originating from "commandments" imposed by an outside authority; rather, it feels like it emanates from our innermost being. That is not to say all religious precepts are correct, for many are no more than derivations from more variable and superficial sources (identified next). Here I am affirming the tried-and-true religious concepts that have prevailed throughout millennia. Thus religion does two things: It explicates the innate moral sense and objectifies it, making it into an external absolute that, in turn, is reinternalized. This becomes the *conscience*, what St. Thomas Aquinas called the moral life "according to reason."

### Level 3—Extrinsic Objective: Social Contract, Education, Laws

These moral universals are further institutionalized within a culture through its social norms, education, and legal principles. *Importantly, it is at this point that they can conceivably be severed from their religious roots.* But that is not to say that we are ever fully independent of these religious antecedents, because historically we still owe much to the preceding religious traditions. And for the majority of people, the religious explication remains the foremost presentation of these universals.

The problem is that, as many informed observers have acknowledged, conceptions of right and wrong can differ from culture to culture.

Anthropologist Ruth Benedict made a statement suggesting that morality is highly relativistic: "Morality differs in every society, and is a convenient term for socially approved habits." Further, we know from our own modern Western culture that institutionalized education does not as a rule teach ethics, values, or morality. Thus cultural institutions face the constant challenge of maintaining and imparting the moral universals.

### Level 4—Extrinsic Subjective: Parenting, Peer Group Norms

This is the level that most closely touches the individual and is the most susceptible to arbitrariness. These are the most subjective and primal influences, especially peer group norms, where we tend to participate in several groups concurrently. This is the most immediate influence between moral principles and behavior, and where the greatest variability manifests.

In fact, there is no guarantee that any ethical learning takes place here. The question is whether these more relativistic sources of values contradict the objective and universal precepts, which they often do. Ultimately, the most desirable outcome is for this dimension to reflect the moral imperatives found in the Extrinsic Universal and Extrinsic Objective levels.

### Level 5—Intrinsic Subjective: Genes

I included genetic influences because there are real and tangible correlations between genes and behavior of all kinds. While there are few hard-and-fast findings, epidemiological studies have shown that certain traits and behavioral characteristics with moral implications have genetic correlations. For example, substance abuse has a strong genetic component and is highly correlated with bad behavior. Thrill-seeking and anger, two characteristics with genetic underpinnings, can also potentially result in antisocial behavior.

Note, however, this is not a deterministic argument for the genetic basis for good or bad behavior. In the studies cited previously, it took *both* bad genes and a bad home environment, not either variable alone, to result in aggressive behavior. Genes did not make these people antisocial; their genes only made them susceptible. Despite genetic influences, it is clear that, with few exceptions, our moral temperament remains well within our control on both an individual and social level.

## Can We Be Good without God?

It would seem that our innate moral sensibility obviates the need for religion. But it actually makes the role of religion all the more important. The "moral language" as described by Hauser and other evolutionary psychologists is inchoate, amorphous, and abstract. Religion for millennia has been humankind's most important moral intermediary between our selfish imperatives and our ethical behavior. That internal moral sense requires external articulation and reinforcement. And throughout history the closest we have come to a formal moral education has emerged from exposure to religion. The other sources of morality (education, parenting, legal system, cultural norms, peer groups) are variable and insular, and usually not appropriate for the development of universal moral principles.

Every atheist will say, correctly I think, that it is entirely possible for a nonreligious person to be moral. But to say that we can have a vibrant moral culture independent of religion is true in only a narrow sense. I believe we can hypothetically eliminate religion and still have a strong moral tradition in place, subject to three qualifications:

1.  This transition to a religion-free culture can happen only if there is a determined, collective effort to replace religion with an explicit commitment to formally teach ethics to children via parenting and educational institutions to a degree that at this point does not exist in any sector of our society.

2.  We must not forget that whatever ethical culture prevails today in our secular society was formed over centuries of religious moral education as an antecedent.

3.  This hypothetical exercise does not apply to most of the developing world, where the educational and legal systems and their corresponding institutionalized moral teachings are considerably underdeveloped.

I do believe that atheists have the same moral capacity as religious people. But whether that capacity is fully actualized is another question. I am also sure that atheists Sam Harris and Richard Dawkins are genuinely ethical people. I do not know them personally, but I am prepared to wager that they have lived privileged lives of familial stability, higher education, financial security, and the luxury of a contemplative life. The rest of humanity, however, is not so fortunate. It is easy for these culturally well-endowed atheists to conceive of a moral life apart from religion, leading them to naïvely suggest that all people can live moral lives without religion.

But I am afraid that while taking religion out of the moral equation may mean fewer acts of martyrdom among a few thousand people, it would also leave a huge moral vacuum for billions more. I do not believe, as Dostoevsky did, that without God everything is permitted. But it is wishful thinking and not consistent with empirical findings that people will act just as morally without religion as they do with religion. Look around—outside of religion, where does the average child formally learn about morality? Religion is the only cultural institution intrinsically committed to the moral improvement of humankind, which cannot be said of education, government, or business.

Atheism by itself does not motivate people to do bad things, but it is lacking one hugely important moral dimension. In our modern secular society, many moral values have already been institutionalized and on some level we can possess these values apart from the religion that developed them. These values will not disappear if we eliminate religion, but the infrastructure that has held those values aloft will substantially weaken. Of all the cultural templates we have, religion is the most robust and explicit about moral behavior.

People of faith have often insisted that in the absence of God human morality would cease to exist. At one point in time that was probably true. Atheists like to point out that we can learn morality from secular sources. But none of those insights, let alone the Enlightenment itself, is remotely conceivable apart from the religious contexts out of which they developed. Ultimately, militant atheists want the moral benefits of religion, but without the religion (as many people want the taste of chocolate without the calories).

In other words, eliminating religion from the cultural morality equation can take place only under rarified and highly qualified conditions. For most people under most circumstances, religion remains the primary model for morality. The innate moral sense by itself is necessary but not sufficient. There is an additional need for a codification and articulation of this moral sense through culture, a process taken up historically by religion. The conclusion is that we are hard-wired to know the difference between good and bad, but religion helps people make that distinction in a way that fosters a moral society.

## The Moral Implications of Science

Time and again I have stated that science is not a moral teacher. However, while the scientific method may be values-neutral, scientific theories and the framework in which they are understood have existential implications, which, in turn, have moral implications.

In fact, allowing science to determine ethics may lead to some very disappointing consequences. With no transcendent and objective claim to moral standards, scientific materialism has no claim to the moral high ground. Imagine the moral philosophy that might naturally flow out of such images as selfish genes, survival of the strongest and smartest, and the view that humans are a dispensable offshoot of blind evolutionary processes, not the pinnacle of anything. How Sam Harris or Richard Dawkins can believe that from reason and science alone we can derive truly humanistic values escapes me.

## Scientific Materialism and Relativism

What might we be saying in and through our scientific materialist understanding of human life? Compared to the idea originally derived from the religious conception that man was made in the divine image, the scientific view says that man is an animal and can be compared to other animals in moral terms. In the traditional evolutionary view, there is no difference between humans and animals, since both are driven by the same survival and gene-replication imperatives. On the plus side, this may lead many people to respect all living creatures. On the negative side and in the extreme, this can yield species relativism: the idea that humans are not the pinnacle of creation; we are no different from other creatures. Indeed, science's revelation that humans are nothing special may in fact lead away from the principle of the absolute sanctity of human life. If we needed proof that an atheistic view of morality can result in diabolically flawed relativist ethics, one should look no further than the Princeton philosopher Peter Singer.

Because humans are a product of evolution, Singer claims that humans exist on a continuum that includes other mammals; thus, there is not a clear separation between humans and animals, which has implications for ethics. One implication is that animals should be treated with greater respect, a point of view that we humans are increasingly and properly coming to share. But the second implication is very disturbing. If humans are animals and our lives are not divinely inspired, the edifice of Judeo-Christian morality about the sanctity of human life is discredited. God is dead and we should recognize ourselves as Darwinian primates who enjoy no special status compared to other animals. Therefore, not only are abortion and euthanasia permissible, but so might be infanticide. While Singer is clearly driven by compassion, his relativist positions derived from his atheistic conception of human life are morally offensive.

Singer has written that "Human babies are not born self-aware, or capable of grasping that they exist over time. They are not persons." And on the viability of the unborn, he has this to say: "The calf, the pig and the chicken come out well ahead of the [human] fetus at any stage of pregnancy, while if we make the comparison with a fetus of less than three months, a fish would show more signs of consciousness." Because, according to Singer, "it does not seem wise to add to the burden on limited resources by increasing the number of severely disabled children," he says that the parents, together with their physicians, have the right to decide whether "the infant's life will be so miserable or so devoid of minimal satisfaction that it would be inhumane or futile to prolong life." Thus, once killed, a disabled infant will be freed of pain. Singer has also written, "Characteristics like rationality, autonomy and self-consciousness make a difference. Infants lack these characteristics. Killing them, therefore, cannot be equated with killing normal human beings." And on killing newborn infants: "I suggest that a period of 28 days after birth might be allowed before an infant is accepted as having the same right to life as others."

I like the idea of treating animals more like humans, but am morally repulsed by the idea of treating humans more like animals. Not all atheists are so morally compromising, of course. But I can't help thinking that, if Peter Singer believed in God and the corollary that every one of us is made in God's image, he would have more respect for the sanctity of human life and would not so easily make his own determinations about what constitutes a worthy person. Singer is probably an unusual case, but it does call up the need for an absolutist dimension of ethics that has historically come from religion and a belief that life is a gift from God. The irony is that Singer is a professor of bioethics.

In the end, knowing that morality is an evolutionary adaptation shared with chimpanzees and social insects does not make a person more likely to act with high ethical standards. However, knowing that such morality is handed down by a higher power that loves him does make a believer more inclined to behave morally, and not so much because he will be punished or rewarded, but because he wants to share in that higher power's goodness. The most powerful way to participate in that higher value is by behaving in a way consistent with that goodness.

## Social Darwinism and Eugenics

According to biologist E. O. Wilson, our whole system of values, including beliefs, virtues, and the rules related to them, is purely a product of evolutionary expediency. In *Consilience*, Wilson says that the insights of neuroscience and evolution will increasingly illuminate morality and ethics in a way that leads "more directly and safely to stable moral codes" than would the dictates of God's will.

I have serious doubts about this claim. Just ask yourself what ethical lessons emerge from the contemplation of this statement by Richard Dawkins: "We are survival machines—robot vehicles blindly programmed to preserve the selfish molecules known as genes." How does that inspire anyone to be more compassionate and charitable? In an instance of self-reflection, Dawkins himself has questioned the validity of a moral system derived from evolutionary science: "A good case can be made that a society run on Darwinian lines would be a very disagreeable society in which to live." In fact, Dawkins has further stated, "If you wish to build a society in which individuals co-operate generously towards a common good, you can expect little help from biological nature. Let us try to teach generosity and altruism, because we are born selfish."

For over 100 years, Darwinism was associated with a particularly harsh and unpleasant view of human nature. And as we have seen historically, social Darwinism has deleterious implications. Whether Hitler was actually influenced by social Darwinism is not important. What is important is that a pernicious relativism is easily derived from the application of Darwinian thought to human affairs.

Social Darwinism is the theory that competition among individuals, groups, nations, or ideas drives social evolution. The term draws upon Darwin's theory of natural selection, where competition between individuals drives biological evolutionary change through the survival of the fittest. If humans are not the result of God's will but of a survival-of-the-fittest gene-replication mechanism that cares not for human life, then there is little rationale to help those who have the misfortune of not being capable of survival on their own: the poor and helpless. The theory implies that those who cannot defend themselves should perish so that evolution can work its species-changing magic.

Certainly, evolutionary science is not responsible for these things: science is values-neutral. But this is what happens when science is allowed to infiltrate moral values without any ethical intervention or interpretation. This is what happens when science is not balanced by values-affirming disciplines such as religion.

## Conclusion

It is clear that science by itself cannot lead to a moral culture. Science has no moral valence. Right and wrong do not come from physics or chemistry or biology. It requires the intervention of ethical institutions, mainly religion. Chris Hedges stated, "It is impossible to formulate a moral code out of reason and science. As the realm of fact rather than value, science is unable to generate a basis for moral behavior. Neither science nor reason calls on us to love our neighbors as ourselves, to forgive our enemies, or to sacrifice for the weak, the infirm or the poor."

The biggest realization for me is that we cannot put our faith in a *relative* truth. Imagine believing in something that depends on something else that depends on something else, and so on. That is not how our minds are organized. We look for that *one* thing that all other things are dependent on. Call it first cause or the cause of causes. This imperative permeates all human strivings, but only religion offers it in a systematic and structured way. If moral imperatives are not instilled as a part of God's will, and if they are not in some sense *absolute,* then moral relativism is the norm.

It is true that today we can extract these moral imperatives and separate them from religion, but that is only after many centuries of a process of externalization and internalization that I have already described. I think it is clear that for the majority of people there seems to be no way to fashion a complete moral architecture excluding religion. My main proposition is that the innate moral sense requires a medium for its articulation and institutionalization, and for most of human history religion has served that purpose.

Religion is uniquely suited to provide the psychological and social context for the necessary consensus about core humanistic values. Religion is uniquely capable of promoting the belief in a transhuman moral authority, thus supporting the ongoing traditions that form the foundation for an ethical civilization.

At some point in our history we transitioned from *human being* to *being humane*. Making that transition was facilitated by religion, the concept of being created in the image of God. And even though I do believe we have progressed as a moral species, it is still too early to dismiss religion.

# Religion Is Union with the Divine: Salvation, Transcendence, and Apotheosis

For thousands of years, human narratives in the mystical tradition have varied in language, idiom, and cultural context, but in essence what is communicated is the same: union with the supreme God, Brahman, Allah—what I prefer to call the *Absolute*. This is not absolutism in the sense of "ideological totalism," but in the sense of infinite worth.

In this chapter, I am taking an excursion into mysticism, but it is important to keep in mind that union with the divine is at the heart of every religion. I think that the need for the infinite and eternal is deeply rooted. We are all aware that the word "God" and its many synonyms are used to refer to the highest expression of human strivings. But I have found that the concept of "God" is not sufficiently broad to describe what is going on in religion, both Western and Eastern. That is why I propose using the term Absolute Value.

## The Quest for Absolute Value

Rudolf Otto, in his masterful *Idea of the Holy*, wrote, "'Holiness' is a category of interpretation and valuation peculiar to the sphere of religion." I think this accurately describes the nature of religion, which in every way is about *value*. Everything about religion flows from this—from the transcendent value we ascribe to the divine to the moral values that define the good life to the worthiness we experience in a relationship with God. Transcendence is the core domain of religion that cannot be provided by any other human institution.

To Paul Tillich, "absolute," from the Latin *absolvere,* "to loosen," means being detached or freed from any limiting or particular relation. It is that which is not relative to or dependent on anything else. St. Anselm, the eleventh-century Archbishop of Canterbury, offers what I consider the most perceptive definition of God as Absolute in his *Proslogion*. He says it is "that than which nothing greater can be conceived."

Here are some additional conceptions of the Absolute:

Plato from *Phaedo*: "When the soul returns into itself and reflects, it passes into the region of that which is pure and everlasting, immortal and unchangeable."

Daisetz Suzuki on the Buddhist conception of Nothingness: "There is no time, no space, no becoming, no-thing-ness; it is what makes all things possible; it is a zero full of infinite possibilities; it is a void of inexhaustible contents."

William Blake from *The Marriage of Heaven and Hell:* "If the doors of perception were cleansed everything would appear to man as it is, infinite."

Empedocles: "God is a circle whose center is everywhere and whose circumference is nowhere."

Meister Eckhart on God: "His simple nature is regarding forms, formless; regarding being, beingless; regarding becoming, becoming not; regarding things, thingless; and therefore He escapes from things of becoming, and all such things there come to an end."

The Maori people of New Zealand conceived of a deity named Io: "He is Io-the-unseen-face, Io-the-everlasting, Io-the-immutable, Io-the-parentless. He is the origin of all things and he has retained for himself the spirit and the life and the form. There is nothing outside or beyond him, and with him is the power of life, death and godship."

From the *Egyptian Book of the Dead:* "God is One and alone, and none other exists with Him; God is the One who has made all things. He is eternal and infinite; He has endured for countless ages, and He shall endure to all eternity."

Chuang Tzu on the Tao: "Do not ask whether the Principle is in this or that; it is in all beings. It is on this account that we apply to it the epithets of supreme, universal, total. It has ordained that all things should be limited, but is Itself unlimited."

The American philosopher J. N. Finlay wrote in *Ascent to the Absolute:* "An Absolute is self-existent, of prime category, without alternatives, intrinsically capable of displaying itself in alternative contingencies and in fact capable of displaying itself in all such contingencies, not confronted by rival Absolutes or by contingencies external to itself, and embodying in the highest conceivable perfection all the values that are intrinsic and mandatory."

There you have it: numerous ways of trying to define the Infinite. Not being religious, I do not make a huge distinction among the various modalities of the Absolute. I recognize that for believers these distinctions are paramount, but for me it is the commonality-among-differences that is so fascinatingly important. So for the purpose of this analysis, it does not matter whether a person believes in an omnipotent and omniscient creator-God who answers prayers and intervenes in this life or a person believes in a changeless, ceaseless, infinite Ultimate Reality that is present in all things, all times, and all beings and is beyond the world of appearances—to me, they are equivalent expressions of man's need for Absolute Value.

Most atheists will say they can do without the "infinite," but I assert this is the core of what it means to be human—and, by extension, religious. In essence, I am saying that we are, even the atheists among us, *homo religious*. It's just that atheists cannot believe in God. Scratch the surface and you will find that all atheists want to believe in some form of the Absolute.

What is fascinating about the concept of infinity is that we cannot ever embrace or define it, but we still know what it is. We can still *feel* it. That does not mean infinity exists, however. But the need for infinity is very much a part of our emotional makeup. The notion of infinity is the essence of the human experience of transcendence.

In religious terms, by Absolute Value I am not only referring to monotheism. I do think that monotheism is the clearest version of Absolute Value, but it really harks back to my original definition of *religious:* the embrace of a Transcendent Spiritual Reality, which can also manifest as pantheism or polytheism. I prefer to use the term Absolute Value in this chapter because it is broader than the concept of Transcendent Spiritual Reality. It applies to all people, not just those who are religious; further, it refers to the *experience* that I believe is at the heart of the human condition. Transcendent Spiritual Reality is the divine entity that religious people embrace to experience Absolute Value. But all people seek Absolute Value, even secularists who don't believe in a god.

All religious traditions express the universal human concern with Absolute Value. Since what people regard as values are strongly influenced by their own temperaments, cultures, and histories, it is not surprising that there are different images of the Absolute. But these traditions all see human life as finding its true fulfillment in a union with such an Absolute.

I therefore present the five necessary attributes of Absolute Value:

- **Intrinsically Good:** Righteous, life-affirming
- **Transcendent:** Above all other reality, the most real
- **Eternal:** Infinite, permanent, undying
- **Universal:** All-inclusive, limitless
- **Unconditional:** Perfect, irreducible, not dependent

This leads to the one question that has persisted in my mind: Where did the idea of Absolute Value come from? It may be argued that we seek Absolute Value because there truly exists an absolute in the form of God. And this is a legitimate claim that I cannot disprove. But my personal feeling is that the "human condition" places upon all people the need to participate in the highest values and ideals we are able to envision. Religion is not the only realm in which humankind finds values; indeed, all culture is a manifestation of our need for values. But religion is the only area in human life where the attainment of Absolute Value is not only possible, it is assured.

## The Religious Dialectic: Separation and Union

One of the most important realizations is that religion addresses an existential human *dialectic* or coincidence of opposites. This takes the form of a negative pole (separation from God) and a positive pole (union with God). I believe this dialectic defines the central organizing concept of all religions: temporality, fallibility, and mortality on one side; eternity, perfection, and infinity on the other side. All religious mythology strives to explain how we were made *human*—why we are imperfect; why we die; why we live in the midst of evil—and how we can be made *divine* (again).

## The Discovery of My Nothingness

Imagine if an adult human being came into existence fully conscious and devoid of any social or cultural constructs, as existentially naked: What would be his experience of the world? His awareness leaves him completely open to experience a world that is expansive and extensive, crushing and commanding, overwhelming and overpowering. His first feeling is not consciousness of his self, but of the vast and extraordinary "other." At this primordial moment, man's openness engenders the perception of a cosmos that is transcendent, superlative, boundless, eternal, inscrutable, and miraculous.

This is what Rudolf Otto called the experience of the *mysterium tremendum* in the face of the transcendent numinous: the total force of the universe as it weighs down upon man. Man finds himself as the infinitesimal surrounded by the infinite. (Pascal: "I see nothing but infinities on all sides, which surround me as an atom.") The world is everything; man is nothing. ("I am naught, thou art all.") The world is omnipotent; man is powerless. (Max Stirner: "How little man is able to control. He must let the sun run its course, the sea roll its waves, the mountains rise to heaven. Thus he stands powerless before the uncontrollable.")

The encounter with the numinous inspires fear, awe, wonder, horror, and dread. Man's relation to the numinous is one of humility, subjugation, sacrifice, and devotion. It becomes an object of worship, veneration, idolatry, and homage. The natural feeling standing before the daunting and annihilating awesomeness of the *mysterium tremendum* is self-loathing, self-depreciation, helplessness, and inferiority.

Man's experience of the *mysterium tremendum* becomes his experience of God. This translates into what Otto has termed the experience of *creature consciousness*, which is "the emotion of a creature, submerged and overwhelmed by its own nothingness in contrast to that which is supreme above all creatures." The creature exists as contingent existence, as nonexistence. Meister Eckhart says: "All that is created has no truth in itself. All creatures insofar as they are creatures are not even illusion, they are 'pure nothing.'"

Creature consciousness is basically the experience of a separation from God, which is defined as the ground of all being, as man's true essence. Thus we read in an Egyptian text: "God is life, and through Him only man liveth. He giveth life to man and he giveth the breath of life into his nostrils." But as a creature, man's *causa essendi* lies outside of himself. There is a gaping chasm between God the creator and man the creature: It is the difference between all and nothing, between absolute plenitude and abject emptiness. This feeling was captured by Emil Cioran: "If God once announced that He was 'that which is,' man, on the other hand, might define himself as 'that which is not.'"

If God is the All and man is outside God, or not God, then man is pure negativity. As such, man is alienated from his true nature, from what he essentially is. The creature depends wholly on something outside itself and is thus nothing in itself. Tillich: "Man as he exists is not what he essentially is and ought to be. He is estranged from his true being." It is a feeling of nothingness in the face of overwhelming being. Otto again: "To the creature is denied, not merely efficacy as a cause, but true reality and complete being, and all existence and fullness of being is ascribed to the absolute entity, who alone really *is*."

This creature feeling is behind the Old Testament experience of Yahweh as a wrathful God. Militant atheists frequently point to the wrathful God of the Old Testament, which they characterize as a spiteful, vindictive deity. But this is not a characterization of God's temperament; it is a characterization of *how man feels about himself*. It is not so much that God is cruel or vindictive; rather he treats man the way he really is: a fallen being, a creature deserving punishment. If God is *prima causa* of all that is, then the creature has its causation outside of itself; is nothing in itself; is a nonentity that is worthless, transient, and perishable. As Otto observed, "There is the feeling of one's own submergence, of being but 'dust and ashes' and nothingness."

You may question whether this is a real human experience. Surely anyone who feels this way would be very depressed, and yet most people around us appear quite content. That is because we are born into cultural structures—family, tribe, society, religion—that counter this "creature feeling" fairly well. It is only when these structures break down that we can become unhinged and existentially naked before the majesty of creation. Rarely does this happen all at once, but I aver that the "creature feeling" is always in the background, behind all defense mechanisms. Most of us do a good job finding higher values— "something greater than ourselves"—to embrace. And I submit that the highest value of them all is the divine.

Ultimately, we seek to unite with some version of the divine to complete the dialectical circle: to transition from nothingness ("dust and ashes") to an apotheosis of man. And as I will show, no cultural institution gives expression to this dialectical process better than religion. This is the "benefit" of religion that has no secular comparison because no mundane existence can transcend human limits. It cannot be provided by any secular belief system. *And this is the pure genius of religion:* to convince ourselves that the finite and perishable world we inhabit is not the real world and that the more real world awaits us after a transition to a more hallowed state.

The Hindu encounter with the Holy in *Bhagavad-Gita* is similar. Krishna, a divine manifestation in human form, has appeared to Arjuna, who says to the God: "O Infinite Being, Lord of the gods, refuge of the universe, Thou art the imperishable, the being and the nonbeing and what is beyond that, boundless in power and immeasurable in might, Thou art All. Seeing thy great form, the worlds tremble and so do I, my innermost soul trembles with fear and I find neither steadiness nor peace."

## The Significance of the Fall

This sense of being wholly separate from the Holy, the sense of not-being, is felt as a pervasive sense of "wrongness," of being out of place, of alienation. The brief section of Genesis outlining the Fall is an attempt to explain, in mythic form, this experience of separation from God. Genesis (1:31) tells us that "God saw everything that he had made, and behold, it was very good." The implication is that God is the source of only what is good. The Garden of Eden and the Tree of Life epitomize this state of goodness. And it is into this state of perfection that God places man. Aside from the Tree of Life, there was also the Tree of Knowledge of Good and Evil. God instituted one command: that man cannot eat of this latter tree. The Tree of Knowledge symbolizes man's freedom of choice between the good (obeying God's word) and evil (disobeying God's will). By eating of the tree, man had in essence chosen evil.

We see here that the inner sense of "wrongness" quite naturally leads to the notion, "I have done wrong." This is understood as the Original Sin. Psalm 51 reads in part: "Against thee have I sinned, and done this evil." Sin is the transgression of God's word. God is the ultimate ground of all being, the essence of the self, the supreme reality. In disobeying God, man severed his relationship with God. Man becomes the incarnated contravention of the Divine Word. In God's sight, man becomes guilty, profane, unworthy.

Sin and death are woven together as they are both the ultimate separation from God. Thus in the biblical context, death enters human experience synonymous with sin. Thereafter man stands naked before God, which is a symbol for his spiritual emptiness, having lost his intimacy with God. This led Old Testament scholar Walther Eichrodt to write, "It is not indeed the simple fact of dying which is here proclaimed as the punishment of sin but the enslavement of all life to the hostile powers of death—suffering, pain, toil, struggle." Thus we understand the origins of mortality, suffering, evil, and human limitations. Man becomes worthy of punishment, of the "human condition": "cursed is the ground for thy sake; in sorrow thou shalt eat of it all thy life. In the sweat of thy face shalt thou eat bread, till thou return unto the ground; for out of it wast thou taken: for dust thou art and unto dust shalt thou return." (Genesis 3:17, 19) The result is travail, pain and death—in short, man's creature status and the rift between man and God.

I want to be clear that this existential sense of *negation* is far more profound than just an encounter with mortality. Ernest Becker, author of the *Denial of Death*, did a wonderful job showing how mortality drives the human animal. But I always felt that his notion was too limiting. Rudolf Otto's idea of "creature consciousness" is a deeper and richer concept. It certainly includes the awareness of mortality, but it encompasses so much more. At its root is the ability of the human mind to conceive of the Infinite. It's a wonderful paradox: on the one hand, we cannot really grasp the Infinite (try counting to infinity some time), yet we can conceive of "that which none is greater," with the additional understanding that whatever the Infinite is, we are not it. This makes for the "creature feeling": the feeling that in the face of the infinite we are finite; in the face of the unconditional, we are dependent; in the face of the eternal, we are temporal—in the face of the Absolute we are its negation.

This is the *negative* side of the dialectic: man's nothingness before the Absolute; man's feeling of sin and unworthiness; man's feeling of separateness from the Holy. But this also sets the stage for man's foremost religious enterprise: his deep desire to atone, to be cleansed of his profaneness, to be enveloped in God's love, to become one with God.

## Union with the Divine

As I have explained, the negative pole of the religious dialectic is of separation from God, as represented by the condition of man's guilt, inferiority, and mortality. The corresponding positive pole of the dialectic is the union with God, the condition of man's salvation, transcendence, and apotheosis. The aim of all religion is to liberate man from a form of bondage and unite with the Ultimate Reality from which he originated. It is, in the widest sense, a self-fulfillment and self-actualization, becoming whole, complete, and perfect.

The union with God is the single greatest mandate of religion. As dreadful as the experience of separation from God is, the union with God is experienced as pure joy, exaltation, and rapture. In seeking God's grace, love, and mercy there is talk of ecstasy, beatitude, and unspeakable bliss. This is what all the temples and cathedrals, rituals and ceremonies, mysticism and asceticism, scripture and commandments, prayer and meditation are all about—the various paths and channels to experience, participate in, share, and merge with the Absolute. It is the ascension of man after the Fall.

Paul Tillich states: "The human heart seeks the infinite because that is where the finite wants to rest. In the infinite it sees its own fulfillment." Tillich further teaches, "The feeling of being consumed in the presence of the divine is a profound expression of man's relation to the holy. It is implied in every genuine act of faith, in every state of ultimate concern." And lastly: "Man is driven toward faith by his awareness of the infinite in which he belongs."

And according to Rudolf Otto, "No religion has brought the mystery of the need for atonement or expiation to so complete, so profound or so powerful expression as Christianity." In Christianity, the distance between the human creature and his God is enormous; the unworthiness of the sinner is complete. And yet, Otto continues, "That God nonetheless admits access to Himself and intimacy with Himself is not a mere matter of course; it is a grace beyond our power to apprehend, a prodigious paradox." Christianity is par excellence a religion of redemption. Cynics have overemphasized the dimension of Christianity that defines and condemns sin and transgression, for its true significance is found in the pursuit of salvation, transcendence, and union with God.

In the biblical text, this union is realized in the "new heaven and new earth" wherein God and man dwell together as they did before the Fall: "Behold, the tabernacle of God is with men, and he will dwell with them, and they shall be his people, and God himself shall be with them and be their God." (Revelations 21:3) In this New Jerusalem, we are told, the temple, which has traditionally served as the mediator between an estranged man and his God, will no longer be necessary: "And I saw no temple: for the Lord God Almighty and the Lamb are the temple of it." (Revelations 21:22) There will be a direct communion between man and God, with no more need of an intermediary.

Evil has become the embodiment of human limitation, mortality, and suffering. Biblical teaching reassures us that the present world, infected with evil and its results (suffering and death) will one day be transformed. Final-age purification will result in a totally renewed creation. The saved will enjoy fullness of life on a new Earth: "The world itself will be freed from its slavery to corruption and share in the glorious freedom of the children of God." (Romans 8:21)

Judeo-Christianity looks to the future and anticipates a glorious fullness, a time when creation will be completely perfected. Universal salvation comes from God's generous sharing of what is his alone to give: fullness of life and eternal happiness. The afterlife represents the culmination, fulfillment, and perfection of created being. It is offered as the purest of gifts that needs only grateful acceptance.

The unity of man and God is exemplified in Jesus. In the Christian vision, God unites humanity to the divine being, giving up the divine glory to share in human finitude and suffering, in order that humans can in turn be raised to share in the divine life. After his death, Jesus is raised to the presence of God and so humanity has in him been permanently united with the divine.

Christ is also the savior because he frees us "from the law of sin and death." His resurrection is seen as the foundation for human victory over suffering and limitation. The union means the rescinding of the curse, and the vision continues: "He will wipe away every tear from their eyes, and death shall be no more, neither shall there be mourning nor crying nor pain any more, for the former things have passed away." (Revelations 21:4) Through Christ, people receive the love of God.

For the mystics especially, there is more than a union with God; there is a becoming *one with* God. Meister Eckhart wrote: "God's being is my life. God's is-ness is my is-ness, and neither more nor less." And again: "The eye wherein I see God is the same eye wherein God sees me: my eye and God's eye are one eye, one vision, one knowing, one love." In the mystical union, man becomes the eternal and infinite. Throughout his works, Eckhart insists upon the absolute oneness of creature and creator: "Between man and God, however, there is not only no distinction, there is no multiplicity either. There is nothing but one."

## Body (Separation) and Soul (Union)

The God separation-union dynamic also manifests itself through the body-soul duality. The embodiment of the creature, of course, is the flesh, which is seen in all religions as utterly transient, perishable, impure, profane, and "dust and ashes" compared to the absolute supremacy of the numinous. St. Paul said, "For if you live according to the flesh you will die, but if by the Spirit you put to death the deeds of the body you will live." (Romans 8:13) The soul is the divine within man. Juliana of Norwich, who lived in the fourteenth century, wrote, "Our soul is made to be God's dwelling place; and the dwelling place of the soul is God, which is unmade."

Thus man is dual. According to theologian Eric Mascall, man exists on the borderline "where matter is raised to the level of spirit and spirit immerses itself in matter." Man as matter is body; man as spirit is soul. Rudolf Otto explains that for Eckhart "one and the same man is beheld from two aspects. On the one hand as a creature of time and mortality, of becoming and formation; on the other as he, the same man, is eternally in and with God." Kierkegaard has similarly written: "Man is a synthesis of the finite and the infinite, of the temporal and the eternal." Man in his temporal aspect is the body; man in his eternal aspect is the soul. Plato in *Phaedo* said, "The soul most clearly resembles the divine and immortal, indissoluble and ever-unchangeable, while the body most resembles the human and mortal, the dissoluble and ceaselessly changing."

As body, man is evil, mortal and bound by the limitations of space and time. The body betrays man's creature-likeness: He is a conditioned, determined, dependent being. He is a mere worm. Indeed, Eckhart regarded man's "earthly selfhood," that is, the body, "as of no more importance than a manure worm." Luther similarly referred to the body as a "shameful sack of worms."

As soul, man is godlike, infinite and immortal. Eckhart said, "When God made man, he put into the soul his equal, his active and everlasting masterpiece. It was so great a work that it could not be otherwise than the soul and the soul could not be otherwise than the work of God. God's nature, his being and the Godhead all depend on his work in the soul." The soul is a vehicle to unite with God. Eckhart again: "As the soul becomes more pure and possesses less of created things, and is emptied of all things that are not God, it receives God more purely and is more completely in Him; and it truly becomes one with God and it looks into God and God into it, face to face as it were; two images transformed into one."

In Egypt, the liberated soul, represented as a bird with a human head, soars into the heavens where it becomes a star among stars, a god among gods. In the Egyptian papyrus of Ani we read: "My soul is God, my soul is eternity." Plato similarly says that the soul freed from the body "departs to the place which is, like itself, invisible, divine, immortal and wise, where, on its arrival, happiness awaits it and where it spends the rest of time with God." St. Augustine had likewise said: "The soul's proper abode and its homeland is with God himself, by whom it was created."

## The Eastern Religious Narrative

I am astonished to read time and again how "different" Eastern religions are supposed to be compared to Western traditions. One instance where Eastern religion seemingly exhibits a huge distinction is in its conception of the divine as nothingness or emptiness. But this is not like our conventional notion of nothingness as the opposite of fullness. Rather, it is used to mean that which is above or beyond all subjective or particular categorization. It is *no-thing-ness*. Things are finite; they are contingent and created. The nothingness of Eastern religion is said to be above all thing-ness and above good-and-bad differentiation. It is clearly a version of the Absolute.

I am a Westerner, so it is no surprise that I prefer the Judeo-Christian conception of the Absolute. But "nothingness" is the Eastern way of saying the Infinite—that which is above the world of appearances, above what is limited and separate. For Easterners, nothingness is truly everything-ness; emptiness is plenitude. And although Eastern religions may technically not be theistic—they often do not even use the term God—they still affirm a Transcendent Spiritual Reality of some kind, a nonmaterial or spiritual existence. The core of Eastern traditions, therefore, is the same as in Western religions.

## Buddhism

The Buddha observed in the First Noble Truth that we suffer because as individuals we are *born*. In Buddhist conception, being born is the equivalent to the Christian concept of the Fall—it is a descent into mortality and bodily imperfection. The cause of suffering in this life is the Second Noble Truth: we persist in believing that this world is the real world; we attach ourselves to this world and its things that are ultimately destined to fall apart. Our attachment to this illusion leads to suffering. The way out, the Third Noble Truth, is the liberation and release from the illusory world. In this life such release is realized through enlightenment and the wisdom to understand the true nature of being. On the next level of existence, liberation comes from reemerging with the transcendent love and universal nothingness that is Nirvana.

I do find the ethical dimension of Buddhism, with its emphasis on compassion, to be very appealing, but the core of the belief is to transcend the material reality and reach infinity. The central focus of Buddhism is the impermanence of this world and the pursuit of some form of eternity, and as such it is no different from any other religious belief system. All existing things are transient and caught up in suffering. By detaching from materiality as much as possible in this life—things, possessions, love objects, the body—we can find some peace in this life before we merge with the Infinite Nothingness. The Buddhist concept of Nirvana is parallel to the Western concept of the divine. Buddhism liberates the believer from the pain and mortality of the embodied world by saying that the world is not real. If the material world is an unreality, then death and suffering are also unreal.

The ego or individual is in the Eastern tradition as the body or sin is in Western tradition—they are moral failings that block the person from participation in the divine. Ultimately, the body and the ego are not really real; they are not the true nature of man. By clinging to finite and temporal things, we have separated ourselves from our *real* selves (as in the Christian tradition of the separation of man from God).

The numinous of Buddhism is not Buddha but Nirvana as the realization of Absolute Value. Nirvana can be attained only through snuffing out the flame of desire, even the desire for Nirvana. Nirvana is viewed as the void in which my individual self and world are dissolved. Thus we have deliverance from the world, whose existence is presented as suffering. Nirvana is another word for "emptiness," but this does not really mean extinction or vacuity. It is Absolute Emptiness transcending all forms of relativity and conditionality, birth and death, affirmation and negation. In the Buddhist conception of Emptiness, there is no time, no space, no becoming, no-thing-ness; it is what makes all these things possible; it is a zero full of infinite possibilities; it is a void of inexhaustible contents. Buddhism, therefore, is as much about salvation and deliverance as is Christianity. Importantly, Buddhism is also every bit as dualistic as Western religion. There are two worlds—that which is subject to illusion, ignorance, impermanence, and suffering, and that which is infinite and everlasting.

## Hinduism

Hinduism is very similar to Buddhism, but there are some distinctions. In Hinduism there is a more pronounced emphasis on the Soul (Atman) and its identity with the Transcendent Spiritual Reality (Brahman). In this sense, Hinduism is more like traditional monotheism. But there remains a strong Buddhist flavor. Thus we read in the *Bhagavad-Gita*, "Forsaking egoism, power, pride, lust, anger and possession freed from the notion of 'mine', one is thus fit to become one with the Supreme." As in Christianity, the ultimate goal is salvation. Adi Shankara from *Viveka-Chudamani*: "He who has been liberated in this life gains liberation in death and is eternally united with Brahman, the Absolute Reality." Equation of Soul with the divine is seen in this passage from the *Upanishads*: "The shining immortal Person who is in the heart and, with reference to oneself, this shining immortal Person who is in the body; he, indeed, is just this Soul, the Immortal, this Brahman."

Central to Indian religion is the idea that all reality is included in one supreme Brahman. The eternal Brahman is unchanging, undivided, and immutable. It is no-thing-ness—no distinction, separateness, finiteness, beginning or end, becoming or change. In this tradition, the spiritual path is a manner of realizing that you are part of the Supreme Reality, that you are divine. That part which is the individual ego is an illusion. When you realize that your true self is identical to the one Atman, then egoism and self-interest disappear and you can contemplate all things as part of the Divine Oneness. The message is the same as in other religions: *This* is not the real world; the world which you must be liberated from is suffering and death. Through meditation and self-discipline, you can achieve release from ignorance and suffering, and realize that your innermost self is identical with the Atman. According to the *Chhandogya-Upanishad*, "The Atman, to know whom is salvation, not to know whom is bondage, who is the root of the world, who is the basis of all creation, through whom all exists, through whom all is conceived. He is the real. He is thy self."

Through the enigmatic power of Maya (appearance) there arises in the Atman *avidya*—false knowing, ignorance, deception. Maya superimposes upon the reality of the One Being the deceptive multiplicity of the world. Shankara wrote in the *Viveka-Chudamani*, "It is ignorance that causes us to identify with the body, the ego, the senses, or anything that is not the Atman. He is a wise man who overcomes this ignorance by devotion to the Atman." He further says, "The desire for personal separateness is deep-rooted and powerful. This notion is the cause of bondage to conditional existence, birth and death. It can be removed only by the earnest effort to live constantly in union with Brahman." Thus, as in Christianity and Buddhism, Hinduism is foremost a vehicle for human liberation or salvation.

## Parallel Traditions

Whether in Eastern or Western religion, *this* world is seen as a cosmic demotion from our true, elevated nature. I can be accused of oversimplifying, but my objective has not been to apprehend the particularities of each religious tradition. Rather, I want to understand how these very different traditions are comparable on the deepest level. In my mind, they all convey a similar understanding of the human condition; they just use slightly different concepts to convey the same fundamental ideas of separation and unity, sin and salvation, body and soul, the earthly and divine. The parallels between Eastern and Western religions are more striking than most scholars have realized. The equation of Eastern and Western religious traditions can be portrayed in the following manner:

| Christianity | Buddhism | Hinduism |
| --- | --- | --- |
| Soul | Highest Self | Atman |
| God/Eternal | One/No-thing-ness | Brahman/Isvara |
| Fall/Sin | Ignorance/Illusion | *Avidya*/False Knowledge |
| Body | Body/Separate Ego | Body/Individual Self |
| Salvation/Heaven | Enlightenment/Nirvana | Liberation/*Moksha* |
| Earthly Existence | World of Appearances | Maya |
| Evil | *Dukkha*/Suffering | *Samsara*/Suffering |

*continues*

*continued*

| Christianity | Buddhism | Hinduism |
| --- | --- | --- |
| Moral Behavior | Right Effort | Karma |
| Afterlife | Reincarnation | Reincarnation |
| Jesus Christ | Buddha | Krishna |

## What of Secular Absolutes?

I want to repeat: The need for Absolute Value is a human universal. And it is a need that characterizes the secular person as much as the religious person. It is just that for the vast majority of people, the religious response to the quest for Absolute Value is far more palatable than any secular version, and for good reason. The religious conception is closer to the mark.

Here is the problem for any unbeliever: What in the material world meets the definition of Absolute Value? What in the natural world is Intrinsically Good (life-affirming); Transcendent (above all other reality, the most real); Eternal (infinite, permanent, undying); Universal (all-inclusive, limitless); and Unconditional (perfect, irreducible)?

I think you will agree that nothing in the natural world as we know it can qualify. This leads to one more question: Assuming I am right about the need for Absolute Value, and the fact that nothing in the natural world measures up, does that not imply that God must exist? That is one implication, although not one I subscribe to.

For me, the more personal question is what in the material world can approximate Absolute Value. Alas, for the secularist, there can be no complete substitute for the divine. To be sure, we can live a very satisfying life without the religious conception of the Absolute, but secular absolutes only go so far. I think this is the greatest challenge facing secular humanity: how to embrace the Absolute (infinite, eternal, unconditional, perfect) in a world without God, who is all these things by definition.

No person can live without something they take as an ultimate, unconditional concern; no one can live in a world of pure relativity. Secular absolutes may be felt as transcendent in an experiential sense, but by their very nature they are *finite and limited* in an ontological sense. What secularists identify as "transcendent" can be highly laudable (human rights, the moral imperative, love, artistic expression, knowledge, science, social justice) but also rather laughable (money, recognition, sex, prestige, success) and lamentable (nationalism, ethnicism, fascism, racism, communism, totalitarianism).

The problem with secular conceptions of the "holy" is that at some point they will invariably fail us. As D. H. Lawrence wrote in *Phoenix II*, "Everything human—human knowledge, human faith, human emotions, all perishes." Secular substitutes are rarely fulfilling in the long run. The secular or material world can offer nothing that is truly absolute. Everything is conditional, fallible, limited, and temporal.

The closest that a secular belief can get us to transcendent value is devotion to the well-being of humanity and of the earth. And this is a very worthy goal, one that is highly compatible with the tenets of religious belief. But it cannot get us to the Absolute as I have defined it. It does offer us a universal that is intrinsically good, but not eternal and not unconditional for it relies on man-made precepts. Secular ideals can carry on for many people for some amount of time, but at some point it has to come to an end. Yet God is infinite, and a believer's endeavor to know him and participate in his world cannot ever be exhausted.

The secularists among us might wonder: Do we really need the eternal and unconditional? Why can't we live a modern, authentic existence with the embrace of the finite and imperfect? I think those of us who do so are forced to make it into a virtue because we have no other choice. But I do not know anyone who would actually turn down a life of eternity and perfection. The mundane by definition is temporal and contingent, and thus cannot be a long-term receptacle for our transcendent urge. The defining limitation of secular institutions is that they are incapable of addressing questions of ultimate concern. They are fixed on the here-and-now world that is transitory and limited. In essence, this is an attempt to make something relative into an absolute, which can never fully satisfy our transcendent aspirations. For true atheists like myself, however, it will have to do. And, hopefully, we choose the laudable and not the laughable or lamentable objects of desire.

It is clear that something is lost by subscribing entirely to the secular model. Surely we can understand that being redeemed in the eyes of Divine Goodness, achieving Nirvana after following the Eightfold Noble Path or being cleansed of existential sinfulness through the resurrection of Christ is much more exalting than the enlightenment that comes from completing three years of cognitive psychotherapy. Secular or material absolutes for the most part are pseudo-absolutes. They are fallible and imperfect—yet also human.

Only religion offers Absolute Value as the sages for millennia have defined it. That is why most people are and will always be religious. Science and reason, as I will later explain, cannot take the place of religion. A secular conception of the Absolute may work for some people, but not most. Religion has two objectives: service to God and service to humanity. As secular people, we cannot give ourselves to God, but we can certainly give ourselves to humanity. Humanity may not be infinite, eternal, and intrinsically good, but this is as close to divinity as a secularist will ever get in this world. And here is the true payoff: Since there is no God, it amounts to the same thing as religion anyway—the betterment of humanity.

# Religion Is Deepening the Soul: Mental Health, Happiness, and Longer Life

It seems a reasonable conclusion to draw that if religion offers many psychological, communal, and emotional benefits, then religious experience should translate into greater life satisfaction, resilience, optimism, and physical health. And that is exactly what researchers the world over have documented in hundreds of research studies reporting a direct positive relationship between religious involvement and improved mental health, extended longevity, and even enhanced social health.

## Empirical Evidence Atheists Cannot Deny

Until recently, the realization that religion is correlated with mental health has actually been the opposite of what the scientific community tended to accept. From the early part of the twentieth century until fairly recently, religious behavior was largely seen as maladaptive. Freud came to see religion as a neurotic defense mechanism that mankind needed to outgrow and overcome. And the conviction that religion damages people remains firmly entrenched in the minds of many observers. Psychologist Albert Ellis is on record as stating that "devout and orthodox religiosity is in many respects equivalent to irrational thinking and emotional disturbance. The therapeutic solution to emotional problems is to be quite unreligious; the less religious people are, the more emotionally healthy they will be."

This perspective mirrors the militant atheists' view that religious people are delusional and religious behavior is pathological. Few extremist atheists at this time are prepared to acknowledge that, on the basis of a cost-benefit analysis, religion has been an overwhelmingly positive force in human affairs. But now we have tangible research results demonstrating the health benefits of religion. The gold standard of atheistic truth—empirical evidence—leaves few doubts that religion is good for the health of the individual and society as a whole.

Being an atheist myself, at one point I was also inclined to discount the value of religion in mental health. Like other atheists, I defiantly asserted that believers could not possibly be any happier than nonbelievers (all other things being equal). Understandably, all atheists want to believe we are just as mentally healthy as religionists. It is important to acknowledge, however, that my personal feelings, replete with built-in biases, are decidedly *not* scientific. Rather, a scientific approach would be to look objectively at the believer population compared to nonbelievers and statistically assess their attitudinal and physiological differences. And when we do those calculations—in the form of analyzing hundreds of studies conducted over several decades across all ages, races, and socioeconomic strata—the preponderance of evidence shows that people who believe in God *are healthier*—mentally, emotionally, and physically. No matter how discomfiting it may be to atheists, the empirical conclusion is that people who only believe in a scientific materialist worldview are less fulfilled than those who believe in divine reality.

Older adults in particular who participate in private and congregational religious activities report fewer symptoms overall, less disability, and lower rates of depression, chronic anxiety, and dementia. And studies have empirically shown that religion helps people cope with physical conditions as diverse as chronic pain, breast cancer, serious spinal cord injuries, and bereavement. In fact, three-quarters of all U.S. medical schools now offer courses in spirituality and medicine.

Certainly there are many miserable believers out there and numerous ecstatically fulfilled atheists. It is important to realize, however, that the conclusions in this chapter are based on statistical averages and may not apply to any person individually. These scientific findings overwhelmingly demonstrate that religion is not the cause of neuroses. When all its benefits are added together, religion is probably humankind's most effective and efficient institution for engendering mental health.

Religion is a prominent source for one's sense of purpose and significance, belongingness, inner peace, appreciation, psychological integration, hopefulness, moral inspiration, and self-acceptance. Consequently, religious people develop a more hopeful and optimistic view of life, deal much better with stressful events, and forge principles of morality and charity that make their communities more cohesive, adaptive, and successful. Certainly many of these benefits can also come from secular sources. However, it is the rare institution that can provide all these modes of well-being in one package, so to speak.

Three meta-analyses synthesizing the results of numerous studies were cited by religious scholar Keith Ward:

- In 2003, an analysis by Smith, McCullough, and Poll of over 200 social studies found that high religiousness (at least weekly church or synagogue attendance) predicts lower risk for depression and drug abuse, fewer suicide attempts, and more reports of life satisfaction.

- In 2002, Bryan Johnson and colleagues at the University of Pennsylvania Center for Research on Religion and Urban Civil Society reviewed 498 studies that had been published in peer-reviewed journals. They concluded that a large majority of studies showed a positive correlation between religious commitment and higher levels of perceived well-being and self-esteem, and lower levels of hypertension, depression, and criminality.

- The editors of the *Handbook of Religion and Health* reviewed 2,000 published studies designed to test the relationship between religion and various medical conditions such as heart disease, cancer, and depression. Their overall finding is that religious people tend to live longer and physically healthier lives than the nonreligious.

Justin Thacker, head of Theology for the Evangelical Alliance, said that there should now be no doubt about the connection between religious belief and well-being. "There is more than one reason for this—part of it is the sense of community and the relationships fostered, but that doesn't account for all of it. A large part of it is due to the meaning, purpose and value which believing in God confers."

Martin Seligman, psychologist at the University of Pennsylvania and director of the Positive Psychology Network, summarized decades of research in his book *Authentic Happiness* with the observation that religious people are less likely to abuse drugs, commit crimes, divorce, or kill themselves. Religious people fight depression better and are less affected by divorce, unemployment, illness, and death. Religion instills hope for the future and greater meaning in life. Religion tempers the impact of adverse life events. And religious people contribute to social welfare because happier people overall are more receptive, empathetic, and loving.

## Defining Life Satisfaction

Religion engenders mental and physical well-being through the enhancement of several psychological and emotional factors. What's interesting to note is that each factor identified next works together with every other factor, creating a mutually reinforcing virtuous cycle. Research has found that religion is associated with:

- Meaning and purpose
- Altruism and generosity
- Consolation and coping
- Social connections and fellowship
- Optimism and hope
- Gratitude and forgiveness
- Relaxation and meditation
- Happiness and fulfillment
- Marital satisfaction and family commitment
- Healthy lifestyle choices

### Meaning and Purpose

Religion remains humankind's primary meaning-building system. Indeed, the essence of religion in the broadest and most inclusive sense, as Paul Tillich contended, is *ultimate concern*. Tillich writes that religion "is the state of being grasped by an ultimate concern, a concern which qualifies all other concerns as preliminary and which itself contains the answer to the question of the meaning of our life."

Humans are aware that we are enveloped within a vast universe. And it is important whether we see this universe as uncaring and hazardous or receptive and loving. Thus religion makes an enormous contribution to life satisfaction because it essentially says that humans live in a benevolent universe, one that cares for our existence. Atheists miss the point that the scientific explanation of the universe, albeit awe-inspiring and fascinating, suggests that we are infinitesimal beings surrounded by an infinite cosmos that is indifferent to our existence.

Even when Christians are challenged by the mystery of how evil can exist in a world created by a beneficent God, thinking that there is some purpose to it, even one that we do not understand, lessens suffering. And the more pointless we perceive the world surrounding us to be, the greater our suffering. Belief in God gives people a sense of a higher purpose. It assures people that the universe is in the benign hands of a benevolent and compassionate divine power. It offers a reason for hope and a life-affirming morality. It is not surprising, therefore, that of the 16 studies researcher Harold Koenig identified that examined the relationship between religion and meaning in life, 15 found a greater sense of purpose and meaning among those who were more religious.

Contemplating a world without religion, Theodore Dalrymple insightfully commented that "the absence of religion can have a deleterious effect upon human character and personality. If you empty the world of purpose, make it one of brute fact alone, you empty it of reasons for gratitude, and a sense of gratitude is necessary for both happiness and decency. Without gratitude, it is hard to appreciate, or be satisfied with, what you have."

## Altruism and Health

Traditional religion has always encouraged believers to be altruistic, especially towards strangers. In Chapter 2 we saw that religious people are much more likely than nonbelievers to donate time, money, and other personal resources to helping others. One analysis showed that in the year measured, people who attended religious services weekly gave

2.8 percent of their incomes to charity, whereas those attending less than weekly donated 1.6 percent, and those who never attended gave just 1.1 percent.

Considerable research has further proven that helping others is the ultimate self-help activity. Many studies have shown that the experience of helping others contributes to a sense of meaning and self-worth, and offers healthy rewards. In a survey of thousands of volunteers, Allan Luks, author of *The Healing Power of Doing Good,* found that people who help other people consistently report better health than peers in their age group. Many also say that their health markedly improved when they began their volunteer work.

Bioethics researcher Stephen G. Post presents several studies suggesting a correlation between altruism and health in his book, *Why Good Things Happen to Good People:*

- In one study, retirees over the age of 65 who volunteered were compared with those who did not. Volunteers scored significantly higher in life satisfaction and will to live, and had fewer symptoms of depression and anxiety.

- In a recent study, people who volunteered for 100 hours or more per year were approximately 30 percent less likely to experience limitations in physical functioning compared to nonvolunteers or those who volunteered fewer hours, even after adjusting for health status.

- Researchers at the University of Miami compared the characteristics of long-term AIDS survivors with an HIV-positive group equivalent. They found that survivors were significantly more likely to be spiritual or religious. Moreover, the effect of religiosity on survival was potentiated by "helping others with HIV."

## Consolation and Coping

As a response to the harshness of life, religion offers solace that one cannot obtain from any other source outside one's personal circle of family and friends. For believers, no army of doctors and social workers can equal God's love. We want to believe that human suffering has meaning and a purpose beyond our paltry selves; we want to believe that the events that make up our lives are comprehensible. Perhaps religion hides the fact that we actually control very little in life, but there is nothing wrong in believing that whatever happens to us has a meaning that allows us to bear our sorrows with greater courage and dignity.

Harold Koenig, co-director of the Center for Spirituality, Theology and Health at Duke University, has systematically studied the link between religion and health for more than 20 years. In general, he found that people with strong religious beliefs—no matter what faith or denomination—recover faster from serious depression and are less likely to become seriously depressed. Furthermore, of 68 studies examining the relationship between religion and suicide, 57 found significantly less suicide or more negative attitudes toward suicide among people who are the most religious. This is important because depression is a barrier to healing and good health. "Religion is a coping behavior," Koenig said, "and depression is kind of an indicator of failure to cope."

Research from the University of Missouri-Columbia shows that religion helps many people with disabilities adjust to their impairments and helps provide a renewed meaning to their lives. This survey was so suggestive of favorable outcomes that the researchers concluded religion ought to be incorporated into standard rehabilitative settings for patients with chronic disabilities such as traumatic brain injury, spinal cord injury, stroke, and arthritis.

Another revealing study showed that religious coping behaviors can be as strong as, if not stronger than, nonreligious coping behaviors in improving mental health. A survey of 577 hospitalized medically ill patients age 55 and over examined the relationship between 21 different types of religious-coping behaviors and mental and physical health. Religious coping behaviors that were associated with better mental health included the reappraisal of God as benevolent, collaboration with God, and offering religious help to others.

Another study showed that religious therapy resulted in significantly faster recovery from depression compared with standard secular cognitive-behavioral therapy. The study examined the effectiveness of using religion-based psychotherapy in the treatment of 59 depressed religious patients. The religious therapy used Christian rationales, religious arguments to counter irrational thoughts, and religious imagery.

## Social Connectedness

Another way of looking at the relationship between religion and mental health is the role played by community or group affiliation. Copious research shows that people who are an integral part of a group are more satisfied with their lives. Harvard political scientist Robert Putman in his book *Bowling Alone* drew on huge amounts of data to demonstrate convincingly that "social connectedness matters to our lives in the most profound way." It affects all aspects of health, physical as well as psychological.

Numerous studies around the world have conclusively established that social connectedness is one of the most powerful determinants of well-being. The more integrated we are within our community, the less likely we are to experience colds, heart attacks, strokes, cancer, depression, and premature death from all causes. The reasons that social connections engender greater well-being are manifold, but include physical help in times of need, reinforcement of healthy norms, and the intriguing correlation between "social capital" and enhanced immunity, among other physiological markers for health.

Religiously involved people consistently report greater social support than do people who are not involved with a religious institution. It is well recognized that religion offers numerous opportunities for social affiliation. Indeed, about half of all voluntary associative participation among Americans is worship-related. Religion is a communal experience that helps provide emotional support and motivates healthy living.

In 19 of 20 reviewed studies, Harold Koenig found a significant positive association between religious involvement and greater social support. Moreover, support provided by religious sources appears to be more satisfying and more resilient than support from secular resources. Continued provision of support from religious sources is bolstered by religious beliefs that emphasize the responsibility to care for and support one another during times of need.

## Optimism and Hope

There is ample evidence that religion promotes optimism and hope. In a 12-year study conducted by a Yale public health facility and funded by the National Institute on Aging, almost 3,000 people age 65 and over were sampled from Protestant, Catholic, Jewish, and other religious backgrounds. Subjects were interviewed annually from 1982 to 1989 and again in 1994. Those who attended religious services most frequently reported increased feelings of optimism and happiness and fewer symptoms of depression. The impact was the greatest for people experiencing functional disability due to chronic illness.

In his book *The Link between Religion and Health*, Harold Koenig identified 14 studies that examined the relationship between religiousness and optimism or hope. Of those studies, 12 found a significant positive correlation. A research team including Martin Seligman discovered that people from fundamentalist Christian groups were more optimistic than people from liberal religious traditions. These investigators traced greater optimism to the content of hymns and liturgies of fundamentalists, whose themes tended to focus on joy, victory over adversity, and salvation. In another study cited by Koenig of nearly 3,000 older adults, investigators documented an association between religious involvement and optimism that was particularly strong among subjects who were experiencing the stress of physical disability.

## Prayer and Meditation

During the past 30 years, meditation has been extensively studied as a way of reducing physiological and psychological stress. In one study, researchers examined the effects of an eight-week stress-reduction program based on training in mindfulness meditation. Following participation, compared to controls, the study found that meditation intervention effectively reduced self-reported anxiety and overall psychological distress, including depression.

The similarity between prayer and meditation suggests that the health benefits of meditation should also be experienced by people who pray regularly—including reduced stress, lowered blood pressure, diminished anxiety, enhanced healing, and augmented immune response. Extensive research by Harvard researcher Herbert Benson has shown that prayer and religious imagery can elicit a relaxation or wellness response. And while Benson noted that the wellness response can be elicited using nonreligious imagery, it is a more powerful technique when patients rely on religion. Benson further observed that belief in a life-transcending force seemed to elicit the fullest relaxation response.

Researchers at Duke University examined the effects of religious devotion in more than 4,000 adult participants. Religious devotion was assessed by frequency of private religious activities such as prayer, meditation, and Bible study. They found that the more frequently people participated in devotional activities, the healthier they rated themselves. This study was important because it showed that *private* devotion, which includes prayer, influences health above and beyond the benefits attributable to the social dimensions of religious involvement.

## Gratitude and Forgiveness

Research suggests that a sense of gratitude is associated with psychological well-being and prosocial behavior. For example, one group of investigators developed a six-item gratefulness scale that they administered along with other measures of positive mental health to 238 college students. Gratefulness was significantly correlated with life satisfaction, empathy, optimism, hope, and prosocial behaviors such as providing emotional and tangible support to others. Gratitude has also been associated with many religious variables, including the frequency of religious service attendance, reading scripture, frequency of prayer, and having a personal relationship with God.

Forgiveness is associated with many measures of wellness. Several studies have demonstrated correlations between forgiveness and better physical health and immune function. Investigators also found forgiveness predicted less frequent substance abuse and reduced antisocial behavior. Forgiveness, in turn, is strongly correlated with religious devotion. One study analyzing data from a national sample of 1,030 Americans aged 18 and older measured several dimensions of forgiveness and religion. The investigators concluded that "the more overall religious one is, the more forgiveness one reports."

## Happiness and Fulfillment

William James was well before his time when he averred in 1902, "Happiness! Happiness! Religion is one of the ways in which men gain that gift. Easily, permanently and successfully, it often transforms the most intolerable misery into the profoundest and most enduring happiness." And when we add up all the aforementioned experiential qualities that religion has been shown to engender—meaning and purpose, altruism, consolation, community and fellowship, gratitude and forgiveness, stress reduction, optimism and hope—the predictable end result is overall life satisfaction.

When it comes to religious attendance, Americans can be divided into three approximately equal-size groups. Surveys analyzed by Arthur Brooks indicate that a third of Americans attend a house of worship at least once a week, while another third attend seldom or never. Brooks calls the first group "religious" and the latter group "secular." (The remaining third attend religious services irregularly.) He found that religious people of all faiths are much happier than secularists. In 2004, 43 percent of religious people said they were "very happy" with their lives compared to 23 percent of secularists. And religious people are a third more likely than secularists to say they are optimistic about the future. Secularists are nearly twice as likely as religious people to say, "I am inclined to feel I am a failure."

And the connection between faith and happiness holds regardless of one's particular religion. Further, it does not matter how investigators measure religious practice. In 2004, 36 percent of people who prayed every day (regardless of service attendance) said they were very happy, versus 21 percent of people who never prayed. In a 2002 study of Protestants and Catholics, researchers found a strong positive correlation between happiness and the intensity of religious belief, level of spirituality, and frequency of coping with life problems through faith.

A recent study in Europe has also indicated that religious people tend to be happier than atheists or agnostics. Lead researchers Andrew Clark of the Paris School of Economics and Orsolya Lelkes of the European Centre for Social Welfare Policy and Research presented their research at the conference of the Royal Economic Society in Coventry, England. The research used data from across Europe to study the impact of religious belief—both the personal practices related to communal faith and to group rituals and communication stemming from shared conviction—on life satisfaction. According to the study, regular churchgoers appeared to cope better with stressful events such as divorce and unemployment. It concluded that the "stress-buffering" effect varies according to the life event and religious denomination, but "churchgoing and prayer are associated with greater satisfaction." Most interesting was the discovery that regular church attendance and an active prayer life lead to greater happiness than passive belief alone.

## Religion and Family

The relationship between religion and life satisfaction is also evident in the circumstances surrounding marriage and children. We know that marriage and family life make for happier people. And we know that religion makes for happier people. Thus it is true that religious people are more likely to be married and more likely to have children than secular people. If we selected 100 adults out of the population who attended religious services every week or more often, on average they would have 223 children among them, according to the 2006 General Social Survey. Among 100 people who attended religious services less than once per year or never, we would find just 158 children.

The marriage-religion relationship also has significant positive implications for the health of society. According to W. Bradford Wilcox, a professor of sociology at the University of Virginia, "Religious faith is linked to happier marriages, fewer divorces and births outside of marriage, and more involved style of fatherhood." Regarding marital happiness, about 65 percent of married Americans who attend church regularly are "very happy" in their marriages, compared to 58 percent of married Americans who rarely or never attend. Religious Americans were also less likely to divorce. Specifically, Americans who attend religious services are about 35 percent less likely to divorce than are married couples who rarely or never attend services. Religion is also linked to lower rates of nonmarital childbearing. Only 25 percent of mothers who attend church weekly had a child out of wedlock compared to 34 percent of mothers who attend monthly or less.

Wilcox's research also reveals that religious fathers are more likely to devote time, attention, and affection to their children than do their secular peers. There are at least three reasons why churchgoing connects men to families: first, the rituals and messages men encounter in houses of worship endow family responsibilities with a higher purpose; second, religious faith helps men weather the stresses of work and family life; and third, the social networks that men encounter in religious institutions tend to keep them focused on the family.

## Important Qualifications

**Is religion the cause or effect?** One obvious question is whether religion merely correlates with life satisfaction or actually causes it. Take church attendance: Are people happier because they go to church or are happier people more likely to attend church compared to less happy people? The correct answer is probably *both*. The association between religion and health undoubtedly works in two directions: religion directly contributes to health, and mentally healthy people are more likely to engage in religious activity. Religion is like a nexus of well-being, operating directly and indirectly through various mechanisms to foster greater life satisfaction. But there is likely a reverse cause-and-effect relationship as well. That is, happy people are more likely to join a community such as a church, mosque, or synagogue; they are more likely to embrace life-affirming values from any source, including religion.

**Is the faith factor a placebo?** The cynical among us may also assert, borrowing from Marx, that religion is the placebo of the masses. But that's not really a pejorative statement since the placebo effect can have a powerful healing impact. Jeffrey Levin, a medical researcher, seems to think so: "The *belief* that religion or God is health enhancing may be enough to produce salutary effects. That is, significant associations between measures of religion and health may in part present evidence akin to the placebo effect." Many passages from religious scripture imply a connection between faith and healing, and while we may not be in a position to confirm the reality of miracle cures, the "miracle" of the placebo effect in religion is probably very real.

**Is it all just positive illusions?** I am an atheist, so my answer is a qualified yes. I do not myself believe in a higher power, so if what we mean by "illusion" is *not real*, then I agree—but without any derogatory implication. In fact, cognitive psychologists tell us that we all live in a world of positive personal illusions, and that our psyches are healthier as a consequence. According to psychologist Shelley Taylor, all of us—*atheists included*—embrace "positive illusions" about our lives to sustain high self-esteem: "People who are confronted with the normal rebuffs of everyday life seem to construe their experience as to develop and maintain an exaggeratedly positive view of their own attributes, an unrealistic optimism about the future, and a distorted faith in their ability to control what goes on around them."

## Physical Health

During the past three decades, numerous researchers studying various populations throughout the world have reported a relationship between religious involvement and enhanced physical health. "Religions package many of the ingredients of well-being to make them accessible to people," according to Richard Eckersley, a fellow at the National Center for Epidemiology and Population Health in Canberra, Australia. And the "psychological well-being that religion promotes is linked to physical health through direct physiological effects, such as neuroendocrine and immune function, and indirect effects on health behaviors, such as diet, smoking, exercise and sexual activity."

The connections among religion, mental health, and physical well-being are manifold. In particular, scientists are studying religion in the context of *psychoneuroimmunology*—the relationship between mind, the immune system, and health. Evidence is mounting of a link between religious faith and mental and physical health through immune mechanisms, more specifically through the activation of the nerves and the release of the hormones associated with improved immune function.

Harold Koenig examined five studies that assessed the association between some measure of religious activity and immune function. In one study of 1,718 older adults who attended church at least once a week, researchers found they were half as likely as nonattendees to have elevated levels of interleukin-6, or IL-6, an immune-system cytokine that indicates inflammation and is involved in many age-related diseases. Lower levels of IL-6 indicate a stronger immune system.

A more recent study focused on HIV patients and found that those with increased religious activity had lower viral loads and higher CD4 counts, another indicator of a stronger immune system. Another study examined correlations between religious involvement and immune function in 112 women with metastatic breast cancer. Importance of religious or spiritual expression was positively correlated with natural killer cell numbers, T-helper cell counts, and total lymphocytes.

## Religion and Longevity

Researcher Harold Koenig reviewed 13 studies conducted between 1993 and 2000 that examined the relationship between religious activity and longevity. Twelve of these studies report a significant relationship between greater religious involvement and longer survival. People with strong religious beliefs have lower blood pressure and fewer heart attacks, spend less time in the hospital, recover faster, have lower mortality rates from cancer and heart disease, and have slower mental decline when stricken with Alzheimer's disease.

Using data from the National Health Interview Survey, researchers found that people who never attend religious services exhibit 1.87 times the risk of death in the eight-year follow-up period compared with people who attend more than once a week. According to the report "Religious Involvement and U.S. Adult Mortality," this translates into a seven-year difference in life expectancy at age 20 between those who never attend religious services and those who attend more than once a week.

In a 16-year mortality study, researchers matched 11 religious kibbutzim with 11 secular kibbutzim (3,900 total members); careful matching was performed to ensure that secular and religious kibbutzim were as similar as possible in characteristics that might affect mortality and controlled for conventional health-risk factors. Of the 268 deaths that occurred, 69 were in religious and 199 in secular kibbutzim, for a mortality difference of 188 percent.

Scientists at Johns Hopkins University, using data from an epidemiologic census of more than 90,000 people, found that less than monthly religious attendance doubled and even tripled the risk of death due to heart disease, pulmonary emphysema, cirrhosis of the liver, suicide, and cancers of the rectum and colon. A follow-up study found a *dose-dependent* inverse relationship between total deaths and frequency of religious attendance. Attending services at least weekly reduced by almost 50 percent the risk of death the following year. Here are the annual death rates according to this survey per 100,000 people by religious attendance:

- Never attended religious services: 2,591 deaths per 100,000
- Attended 2 to 12 times per year: 1,512
- Attended once per week or more: 1,308

Most recently, as part of the Women's Health Initiative (a national, long-term study aimed at addressing women's health issues and funded by the National Institutes of Health), researchers evaluated the religious practices of more than 92,000 post-menopausal women over a 7.7-year period. They discovered that regular religious service attendance reduces the risk of death by approximately 20 percent from all causes. This study was intriguing because, even controlling for the enhanced social support and better lifestyle choices known to be correlated with religious practices, the improvements in mortality exceeded expectations—hinting that there are other factors associated with religious belief and practice that engender improved longevity.

## Fostering a Healthy Lifestyle

Religious people are more likely to engage in healthful behavior and avoid health-endangering activities. Religious involvement has been associated with lower rates of alcoholism, drug use, cigarette smoking, risky sexual activity, failure to wear seat belts, drinking while driving, and other hazardous activities. Investigators looked at 138 studies that examined the relationship between alcohol or drug use and religiousness. Of those studies, 124 (90 percent) reported significantly lower substance use among the more religious. They found a similar pattern with cigarette smoking: of 25 studies that examined a relationship, 24 found less smoking among the more religious. Religiously involved people are also more likely to have their medical illnesses diagnosed early and treated more effectively.

One study reported the results of a 28-year follow-up study of 5,000 adults involved in the Berkeley Human Population Laboratory. Mortality for persons attending religious services once per week or more often was almost 25 percent lower than for people attending religious services less frequently; for women, the mortality rate was reduced by

35 percent. The study found that frequent church attendees were more likely to stop smoking, increase exercising, expand social contacts, and stay married.

In another study, cigarette smoking and religious activities were examined in a six-year prospective study of 3,968 people age 65 and older in North Carolina. Both likelihood of current smoking and total number of pact-years smoked were inversely related to attendance at religious services and private religious activities. If people both attended religious services at least weekly and read the Bible or prayed at least daily, they were 90 percent less likely to smoke than those involved in these religious activities less frequently. This mirrors results from studies of Seventh Day Adventists, which proscribe alcohol, drugs, and nicotine while they prescribe healthful diets and exercise.

## Conclusion

Extensive empirical research has shown that religious affiliation of almost any kind is positively correlated with better mental health, measures of life satisfaction, and prosocial behaviors; which in turn are associated with enhanced physical well-being and healthy lifestyle practices; which are further related to enhanced quality of life and extended longevity.

Militant atheists, it seems, are always claiming that they want to save people from the effects of religion. But save people from what, exactly? Why would they want to "save" people from the enhanced fulfillment, gratitude, optimism, health, and happiness that research proves religion helps to foster?

# Religion Is a Force for Progress: Human Rights, Science, and Universal Ethics

The argument for or against religion's influence in history has to do with the emergence of Western civilization's preeminent secular ideas: democracy and freedom, science and technology, and universal human rights.

My interpretation of history is predicated on two assumptions:

1.   History reveals inexorable progress.
2.   Religion has always been an integral part of Western culture.

These assumptions lead to one inescapable conclusion: Religion has been an essential force in bringing about this historical progress. The alternative perspective is untenable—that without religion we would have gotten here much sooner and/or we would be much further along. While we do not know anything about how history would have proceeded without religion, the most likely proposition is that we arrived at this historical juncture in large part because of religion, not in spite of religion.

In Chapter 2, I discussed religion and morality on the level of the individual. Here I will speak about the collective impact of religion as a historical phenomenon. I do not think it is productive to take a long-and-winding survey of world history and grade religion on its merits and demerits. History is highly malleable to anyone's analysis. In this chapter, I am going to present a selective—but I do not think distorted—view of religions' role in our historical development.

## How We Got Here

The real lessons of history do not pertain to *what* happened—events, dates, and places. Rather, the most important realization is that history is about *how we interpret what happened.* I am not a cultural relativist; I know there is truth out there. But seeking a consensus about that truth is another challenge altogether. I am amazed that two people can see the same accident on a street corner and have two different interpretations of what happened, never mind the myriad conflicting interpretations of something as multifaceted as history.

I think it is naïve to believe that any one of us is capable of looking at history and extracting from any one historic account all the good and bad attributable to any one factor. I have found that three thought biases come into play:

- We oversimplify by focusing on one factor as a major determinant of history to the exclusion of other factors, not realizing that the zeitgeist is much more complex than that.

- We see what our temperament/attitude/ideology makes us see; selective perception reigns supreme.

- We too often engage in simplistic linear thinking: that we can trace the development of one variable to another just by drawing a straight line from one time period to another, and then assume a causal relationship.

Under these conditions, it becomes possible to "prove" any claim about history. However, because there is never a "control group" for any historical period (we cannot see history unfold under different conditions), what we're left with is our own judgment. Of course, that axiom applies to me as well, but with one small difference—I am aware of it.

## Religion: A Force for Good

What I hope to accomplish in this chapter is an interpretation of religion's effects on history that is based more on practical sense and less on ideological preference. Religion is arguably the most powerful and pervasive cultural force on Earth. Throughout history religious ideas and commitments have inspired individuals of faith to transcend narrow self-interest in pursuit of higher values and truths. History shows that acts of love and compassion, self-sacrifice, and service to others are frequently rooted in deeply held religious views. I will argue that, if we have grown as a civilization, of necessity it has been partly because of religion. This does not absolve religious leaders and their followers of responsibility for heinous acts, but it does suggest strongly that religion has had an overall positive impact and that we probably would not have arrived at our current historical destination without religion. Religion did not hold us back; rather, it has been a force pushing us forward.

Several influential religious observers have documented the contribution of Christianity specifically to the rise of Western culture: Rodney Stark (*The Victory of Reason, For the Glory of God*), Gregg Easterbrook (*Beside Still Waters*), Christopher Dawson (*Religion and the Rise of Western Culture*), Keith Ward (*The Case for Religion*), David Noble (*The Religion of Technology*), Alister McGrath (*In the Beginning*), and Robert Royal (*The God that Did Not Fail*). I cannot equal these authors' scholarship, but I will strive to cut through the clutter and provide a revealing overview.

I am as acutely aware as anyone of religion's historical failings. But religion is self-correcting and the intent of this chapter is to look at how religion has become the greatest force for good in the world. It is not only that religion is the most righteous institution, which I believe is true, but that religion is unique in the moral authority it possesses over the world's population to motivate people to good works. And there is no plausible substitute for religion's moral authority.

Simply put, the history of humanity is the development of cultural institutions and their gradual improvement. That is true for government, education, and science as well as religion. Rather than being a force for inertia, organized religion, according to historian Robert Royal, "has been a powerful energizing force in the very development of civilization." Indeed, it is no coincidence that the evolution of Christianity into a diverse and accommodating theology coincided with the development of human rights and democratic principles.

The alternative conclusion, implied by militant atheists, is that we would be further along the progressive trajectory without religion. This is implausible in that historians cannot identify any other cultural force as robust as religion that could have carried civilization forward. One might attempt to argue that science is precisely that other cultural force. But that overstates the power of science to transform the world in a way that is not technologic and economic, which is to say in terms of morality and values (plus art, music, literature, architecture, philosophy, and other expressions of the human spirit). Science by its nature is values-neutral. So outside of religion, there is not any other singular explanation for our progress over the past 500 years.

I may not be a historian or theologian, but I am left with the commonsense notion that somehow we traversed from medieval darkness to modern enlightenment. And if religion, specifically Christianity, was so much a part of people's lives for so long, then religion had to have been more a transformative power than a reactionary force.

## Atheists' Use and Abuse of History

Militant atheists seek to discredit religion based on a highly selective reading of history. There was a time not long ago—just a couple of centuries—when the Western world was saturated by religion. Militant atheists are quick to attribute many of the most unfortunate aspects of history to religion, yet rarely concede the immense debt that civilization owes to various monotheist religions, which created some of the world's greatest literature, art, and architecture; led the movement to abolish slavery; and fostered the development of science and technology. One should not invalidate these achievements merely because they were developed for religious purposes. If much of science was originally a religious endeavor, does that mean science is not valuable? Is religiously motivated charity not genuine? Is art any less beautiful because it was created to express devotion to God? To regret religion is to regret our civilization and its achievements.

Atheists see religion largely through a lens of distorted history. Yet history is so nuanced, multidimensional, and complicated that people can find confirmation for any preconceived conclusion. And atheists generally read history in a way that categorically justifies their condemnation of religion. In the atheist's mind, if a religious person does something bad, it's the fault of religion; hence, religion is evil. If a religious person does something good, it was done for a religious reason and therefore does not count.

Perhaps atheists' greatest misunderstanding of history is their failure to grasp that religion is not a static institution. Religion has evolved with history and history has evolved with religion. Christianity's responsibility for heinous events such as the Crusades and the Inquisition (roughly 700 and 500 years ago, respectively) occurred at a time when religion was essentially a tool of the state. It was also at a phase of religious development that we might call "adolescence," a tumultuous

93

period in the Christian lifecycle that the church has long outgrown. The fact is that a dynamic religion operating in a fluid historical milieu cannot remain unchallenged and unchanged.

The consequence is that Western religion has undergone enormous progress over the centuries and has now reached a more mature phase. Because Western institutions are for the most part *open*, they are self-correcting. No one should condemn any institution solely by the misdeeds of the past, but recognize that over time the good is preserved and the bad jettisoned. And thus it is important to realize that religion in the West has evolved to the point where none of those tragic misdeeds are remotely conceivable today. Religion as an institution has undergone considerable improvements over time and will continue to do so.

Militant atheists mistakenly assume that a world without religion would be much as it is today, just minus the wars, ignorance, and oppression they attribute to theism. In other words, in their ideological view, a world without God would be much more peaceful, fulfilling, and happy. My question to atheists: Could we have gotten this far in history—scientifically, morally, technologically, and culturally—without religion? I believe the obvious answer is "no."

## Religion as a Facilitator

However, I must offer the same criticism to Christian apologists such as Rodney Stark, who has said, "The success of the West rested entirely on religious foundations, and the people who brought it about were devout Christians." To assume we would *not* have gotten here at all without religion is simplistic: It assumes that if religion were extracted from the historical process we would be left with a gaping hole that nothing else would have filled.

I believe in some amount of *historical necessity:* that some ideas are so important and so much a part of human nature that we would have gotten to this point in history anyway, sooner or later. The question, therefore, is whether religion was an impediment or a facilitator. And I still hold that the evidence indicates that religion was likely a facilitator. I think it is very reasonable to assert that, given its enormous influence, religion was a very important factor behind many of our most cherished cultural achievements.

The cultural relativists among you may question whether Western society really is superior to the rest of the world, but in my mind it is impossible to deny that the West has advanced well past other cultures. Most noteworthy is the emphasis on science, technology, democracy, capitalism, and human rights—all ideas that originated in the West and have recently gone global.

For most of Western history, therefore, religion has been a vital and necessary part of the sequence of events we call progress. Atheists maintain that secular institutions and experiences have always stood in opposition to religious institutions and experiences. The reality of the situation reveals a surprising paradox: We owe our most prolific secular institutions largely to religion, which includes the very institutions that challenge the veracity of religion.

It is true that religion may potentiate violent tendencies or intensify conflicts, but more often religion has been a voice of moderation and reconciliation, which has been its stated role. Far from being the biggest source of wars, religion has been the greatest humanizing force in history.

## The Western Idea of Progress

One of the most important Christian contributions to the understanding of history was the notion of linear, progressive time in contrast to cyclical time. "No single idea has been more important than the idea of progress in Western civilization for nearly 3,000 years," writes Robert Nisbet in his *History of the Idea of Progress.* "Simply stated, the idea of progress holds that mankind has advanced in the past—from some aboriginal condition of primitiveness—is now advancing, and will continue to advance through the foreseeable future." According to Nisbet, what Greek and Jewish thinkers began, classical Christian thinkers continued.

> *The Christian philosophers endowed the idea of progress with new attributes which were bound to give it a spiritual force unknown to their pagan predecessors. I refer to such attributes as the vision of the unity of all mankind, the role of historical necessity, and the image of progress as the unfolding through long ages of a design present from the very beginning of man's history.*

Nisbet added: "To these attributes one other must be added: the emphasis upon the gradual, cumulative, *spiritual* perfection of mankind, an immanent process that in time would culminate in a golden age of happiness on Earth, a millennium with the returned Christ as ruler."

Not only was progress an integral part of the Christian idea of history, but because Christianity was so dominant a cultural force, whatever happened within the church necessarily had a wide impact on the course of European history. In one fascinating example, the close relationship between religion and progress can be seen in the development of the King James Bible as described by Alister McGrath in his book *In the Beginning.* Previously the Bible was available only in Latin, which few Europeans could read, thus leaving biblical interpretation to the priesthood. Latin was the language of the church, of diplomacy, and of scholarship—but not of ordinary people. The translation of the Bible in the sixteenth century into the living languages of Europe was a far-reaching development. Finally, the laity could read and interpret the Bible for themselves, rather than rely on clergy. This not only changed the church and religious life, but the wider culture.

This illustration is meaningful because it reveals how influential religion was before the Enlightenment. During the time of the Reformation, Christianity was so pervasive in the lives of ordinary Europeans that any major innovation in the way the Bible was presented or interpreted invariably had a profound effect on their lives. It suggests that progress in Christianity was undeniably integral to the progress of Western civilization, and that it could not have been otherwise. According to McGrath, by the end of the sixteenth century, the dissemination of the Bible helped make the English population "the most literate in Europe." And these "new" translations "sanctioned the right and capacity of people to think for themselves." It may have been the printing press that offered people the opportunity for literacy, but the medium for accomplishing that was the Bible, a development that shook the foundations of the Church and laid the roots for the development of greater intellectual freedom.

The great irony is that out of the intellectual liberalism made possible by Christianity emerged the hugely successful secular institutions we appreciate so much today: democratic government, science and technology, and private enterprise. Western religion allowed for greater freedom of inquiry, and this just snowballed. Greater freedom led to greater inquiry and still more freedom. With the rejection of the authority of the church in the Reformation, greater diversity of thought prevailed in Europe, and a more important role was assigned to the individual in the pursuit of truth.

The divergence of the secular from the religious began fairly early. Thomas Aquinas integrated Aristotle into Christian natural theology. He believed that truth is known through reason (natural revelation) and faith (supernatural revelation). He taught that witnessing the natural world can prove the existence of God and his attributes. The differentiation of theology from natural philosophy (the precursor to science) began in earnest during the tenure of the Oxford theologian Franciscan John Duns Scotus in the thirteenth century. He argued that the theologian and the philosopher study separate subjects and only theologians are qualified to study God, since revelation was a matter of faith rather than natural experience. In time, science was concerned only with natural processes while theology dealt with the nature of God.

Through the Renaissance, this divergence widened, with profound implications. Invariably, the study of nature distinct from the supernatural led to skepticism of the supernatural. In time, philosophy and reason-based science emerged as disciplines distinct from theology, and they began to question the foundations of religion itself.

## Human-Centered Religion: Dignity of the Individual

The significance of this development bears repeating: Christianity helped produce a flourishing secular culture that would eventually go on to challenge the authority of God and emphasize the autonomy of man. As Christianity turned from being God-centric to more human-centric, the basic ideas that took flight centered on *human* reason, rights, equality, and freedom. These ideas emerged from the original Christian concepts that God is a rational creator, all people are made in the image of God, and all people are equal in the eyes of God. And these important notions exist at the root of the major secular institutions upon which the Western world (and, increasingly, the entire world) is based: free-market economics and global capitalism; democracy and plural society; science and technology.

As a consequence, Christianity begat a secular culture that was initially energized by religious sentiments, but eventually took on a thriving existence of its own. Over time, the human-centered secular world pulled away from its religious source. Once the individual and his faculty for reason was liberated from church authority, rational inquiry turned its sights on all forms of belief that might limit the individual's freedom, and this included religion itself.

Interestingly, this "enlightenment" occurred only in the context of Christianity. A commitment to human dignity, personal liberty, and individual equality did not previously appear in any other culture. Freedom in its myriad expressions—of inquiry (science), government (democracy), and economics (capitalism)—first emerged in the West and nowhere else. And to explain their development, one must look at what distinguished the West culturally, namely Christianity. All geographic regions have their affinity religions (Hinduism, Islam, Buddhism), but only in the West did religion "die" and a dynamic secular culture emerge.

To be sure, I believe the principle of freedom would have eventually found its way through humanity, because freedom is an indomitable human imperative. Christianity, with its emphasis on the separate, irreplaceable value of each human soul, emerged as the propitious starting point for what has become an inexorable worldwide trend. So while I think it is incorrect to say that the rise of freedom depended entirely on Christianity, I do think it is fair to say that the freedom imperative was facilitated and accentuated by Christianity.

Western religion developed the innovation of equating the individual with the universal: once we see ourselves as free individuals, and to the extent that we understand that we are all creatures of one God, we understand that freedom and dignity are the right of all people. A religious view of society, at least in the Abrahamic traditions, works on the principle that God created human beings to be free and responsible agents. If human beings are all God's handiwork—and if, moreover, they are made in God's image, as Christians from the early days believed—then it follows that they must all be moral equals. This was an enormous moral achievement because the first human inclination is not to universalism, but to localism. But once my "tribe" is equated with "humanity" through the affirmation that all men are equal in the sight of God, my umbrella expands to encompass all people.

The notions of human dignity and equality have, therefore, a religious derivation. And the distinctiveness of Christianity was to focus on the dignity of common people. We today live in a world where we take for granted the idea that every person deserves equal regard. That archetype was embodied by Christ—a common man of humble roots. He spent his time with the poor and sick. He moved in the everyday milieu of the simple folk. Christ had not come to mankind as an aristocrat, but as a human being of the lowest social station. Thus we read in Galatians (3:28) that "There is neither Jew nor Greek, slave nor free, male nor female, for you are all one in Christ Jesus." If we see God in the other, the other deserves equal respect. This was a concept ultimately shared by Islam as declared by Muhammad, "All human beings are equal like the teeth of a comb. There is no superiority of an Arab over a non-Arab, of a non-Arab over an Arab, of a white man over a black man or of a male over a female. The only merit in God's estimation is righteousness."

No surprise, therefore, that believers were the motivating force for the abolition of slavery. Slavery was the foundation of Greek and Roman civilization, where human life had very little value. Gross inequality was the norm to the point where the lives of most people were expendable and slavery was pervasive.

In the early fifth century, St. Patrick rejected all forms of slavery, the first public person in history to adopt such a categorical stand. And Augustine, in *The City of God*, called slavery an "inconceivable horror."

Of course, at the time, many prominent Christians affirmed slavery, but this does show that there were dissenting voices early on. It would be Christians who eventually deviated from the historic status quo and organized the movement that ended slavery in the West. Given how entrenched slavery was in the world economy and how heinous was the entire enterprise, abolition is undoubtedly the Western world's greatest moral triumph.

That religion played a leading role in the abolition movement is not an exception. Throughout history spiritual conviction has been behind much social progress, including fighting for justice, standing up for the voiceless and the weak, and reaching out in acts of kindness and compassion to the stranger and the outcast. Christians have founded hospitals, hospices, schools, and universities. Invariably, without religiously inspired moral action, the world today would be a place of much diminished humanity. During the depression of 1893 to 1897, religious leaders founded the influential "social gospel" movement, which emphasized New Testament directives that society be restructured with fairness to the disenfranchised. Social-gospel advocacy became integral to the establishment of trade unions, child labor laws, public relief programs, and other reforms. By the arrival of the Great Depression, social-gospel thinking was entrenched in the mainstream among political leaders.

Belief also played an important role in the dissolution of tyranny in the former Soviet Union, with demands for freedom of worship on the part of Catholics and the Eastern Orthodox Church pressuring totalitarian regimes throughout the Eastern bloc. Faith also helped oppose military dictatorships in Latin America, especially under the banner of "liberation theology." And religion continues its campaign against oppression the world over. In Myanmar (Burma), Buddhist monks nearly brought down an evil regime in 2007. And in Zimbabwe, where a brutal dictator has destroyed the lives of millions, Roman Catholic bishops previously distributed a letter, "God Hears the Cries of the Oppressed," in an effort to bring about peaceful democratic change.

Timothy Shah of the Council on Foreign Relations argues that religion has had a profound impact on moving the world toward greater freedom. By his calculations, more than 30 of the 80 or so countries that became freer in the period 1972 to 2000 owed some of the improvement to religion. Sometimes established churches helped push for democracy (such as the Catholic Church in Poland), but more often it was pressure from the grassroots: religious people usually look for a degree of freedom, if only to pursue their faith.

Perhaps most important, religion has been an underlying motive for millions of people whose good works have formed the bulwark for social progress and philanthropy. Religious obligation is one major reason Americans give more to charity (over $300 billion annually) than any other nation measured in the aggregate, per capita or as a percentage of GDP. Throughout American history, faith-based organizations such as the Salvation Army have provided for the poor, reached out to criminals, and reformed addicts and alcoholics. And the collective effect of millions who are inspired to volunteerism, good works, and ethical behavior has helped tremendously with humanity's gravest problems.

## The Religious Origins of Science and Technology

Modern science had its inception in the religious idea that nature was God's creation, and to study it was a way to celebrate God's glory. Aquinas believed that since God created the universe through *logos*, the divine wisdom, the universe must be supremely rational and knowable. Indeed, most of the world's early great scientists were deeply religious: Copernicus was a lay canon of the Catholic Church; Kepler studied the heavens believing that they manifested the wisdom and beauty of God; Newton formulated laws of nature in the belief that the wise author of nature must have ordered the cosmos in accordance with rational and comprehensible principles.

We know science emerged out of religion because before science there was *only* religion. The historical "fossil record," so to speak, proves that science emerged out of religious aspirations. But militant atheists believe we owe the scientific age to a small coterie of enlightened freethinkers who went down a heretical path to discover the laws of the heavens while liberating the spirit of reason from the shackles of religious dogma. As I will show, however, science and technology did not emerge in spite of religion or separated from religion. Rather, all the prominent scientists of the pre-Enlightenment era were religious. The historic point when science emerged as a fiercely independent discipline vis-à-vis religion was probably the late nineteenth century, exemplified by Darwin himself, who began his scientific career as a believer but in the end was seriously questioning his faith. The science-religion divergence became outright conflict when science began to reveal a truth that directly contradicted literal interpretations of religious scripture.

Interestingly, while just 7 percent of elite scientists today claim to believe in God, if we could have performed a comparable survey of the greatest scientists throughout history, the figure may be closer to 75 percent. Consider a list of the 20 most influential scientists in history compiled by John Galbraith Simmons for his book ranking the world's top scientists. His listing spans a period from Nicolaus Copernicus (1473–1543) to Linus Pauling (1902–1993), with most living in the fifteenth to nineteenth centuries. Of the 20 identified, 10 were Christians, 4 were deists, 1 was Jewish, and 5 were agnostic or atheistic. Excluding the scientists born after 1800, *all* the scientists were religious believers. This strongly suggests that in the centuries when science was becoming established, the two disciplines were not polarized antagonists. Science and religion were inextricably related, and the argument can be made that Christianity in particular created an intellectual environment in which science could flourish.

According to Rodney Stark, the spirit of reason was derived from the Christian view that "depicted God as a rational, responsive, dependable and omnipotent being and the universe as his personal creation, thus having a rational, lawful, stable structure, awaiting human comprehension." Among the scriptural passages most frequently quoted by medieval scholars to justify their scientific quest is this line from the Wisdom of Solomon: "Thou hast ordered all things in measure and number and weight." Thus did Tertullian, one of the earliest Christian theologians, instruct that "reason is a thing of God, inasmuch as there is nothing which God the Maker of all has not provided, disposed, ordained by reason—nothing which He has not willed should be handled and understood by reason." And as Saint Bonaventure explained, it is the purpose of science that "God may be honored."

Man embarked on a journey to understand the mind of God by scientifically deciphering the divine design behind nature, which had come to be viewed as a God-crafted mechanism. Even Newton believed that his scientific efforts to discern the operating laws of nature were "directed almost exclusively to the knowledge of God." Newton's religious beliefs encouraged him "to search for divine efficacy in every aspect of the material order." For Newton, to understand the hidden logic of the universe was to understand, and in that sense identify with, the mind of its creator.

I do not want to suggest that without Christian theology, science would never have come into being. The ancient Greeks, for example, questioned the nature of existence long before Christianity. But it is also wrong to suggest that Christianity was only an impediment to scientific development and that science might today be further along were it not for the "reactionary" force that is religion. In my mind it is a matter of religion engendering an environment receptive to innovations in knowledge. And when we compare the West to regions of the world long dominated by other religious traditions, such as Islam and the Eastern religions, we find that the West, with its Christian heritage, has long dominated the realm of scientific thought.

The same is true with technology, which originated as the "practical arts" or "useful arts" inspired by scripture and man's aspiration to reclaim the special relationship with God. Ernst Benz wrote in *Evolution and Christian Hope*, "Significantly, the founders of technology have felt that the justification of the most far-reaching aims of their technological efforts could be found in this very thought of the destiny of man as *Imago Dei* and his vocation as the fellow worker of God … to cooperate with God in the establishment of his Kingdom."

This view of the useful arts as divinely inspired was first articulated in the ninth century in the work of Carolingian philosopher Erigena, who was the first to use the term *artes mechanicae* to denote invention, commerce, medicine, and industry. He argued that the useful arts were part of mankind's original endowment, his Godlike image, rather than merely a necessary product of his fallen state. Thus the mechanical arts had a spiritual significance and an honored place in divine machinations. Through pursuit of the mechanical arts, it was believed, man could progress to perfection, helping to restore him to his state before the Fall. The arts, Erigena wrote, are "man's links with the Divine, their cultivation a means to salvation."

The twelfth century Augustinian canon Hugh of St. Victor likewise linked the mechanical arts directly to salvation and the restoration of fallen man. For Hugh, according to medievalist Elspeth Whitney, "the mechanical arts supply all the remedies for our physical weakness, a result of the Fall, and, like the other branches of knowledge, are ultimately subsumed under the religious task of restoring our true, prelapsarian nature." Hence, "through its relationship to man's final end, the pursuit of the mechanical arts acquired religious and moral sanction." This, then, "is what the arts are concerned with," wrote Hugh of St. Victor, "this is what they intend, namely, to restore within us the divine likeness." This helped to foster in Europe a unique spiritual commitment to the elementary forms of technology.

Technology, in other words, was man becoming godlike. As mankind waited for divine redemption, the useful arts were a means to salvation on Earth. "Providence has decreed," Giordano Bruno wrote at the end of the sixteenth century:

> Man should be occupied in action by the hands and in contemplation by the intellect .... [And thus] through emulation of the actions of God and under the direction of spiritual impulse [men] sharpened their wits, invented industries and discovered art. And always, from day to day, by force of necessity, from the depths of the human mind rose new and wonderful inventions. By this means, separating themselves more and more from their animal natures by their busy and zealous employment, men climbed nearer the divine being.

Francis Bacon also affirmed that the true ends of scientific knowledge and technology is the "restitution and reinvesting of man to the sovereignty and power which he had in his first state of creation." Largely through the enduring influence of Bacon, the medieval identification of technology with transcendence informed the emergent mentality of modernity.

## Moral Progress: Reasons for Optimism

It comes as no surprise that not everyone holds the view that humanity is on a trajectory of progress. Chris Hedges, in his book *I Don't Believe in Atheists*, asserts that the perspective that humankind is on an upward moral trajectory is an illusion. He states that we have progressed economically and scientifically, but not ethically. He argues that there is nothing in human nature or history to support the idea that we are morally advancing as a species. He even makes a predictive statement that I find unbelievable: "The prospects for the human race are bleak." Although Hedges is a moderate who decries the extremism of both the religious right and militant atheism, his perspective is extremely and unnecessarily negative. Since Hedges is not the only cynic out there, I want to address the issue of moral progress.

Certainly we have not made as much progress in the moral realm of our lives as we have in the scientific, economic, and technological realms. But to deny the reality of moral progress is overly cynical and, in my mind, reprehensible. And I am astonished that there are many Americans who believe we are a decadent and evil society; that we have made no moral progress or, worse, we are in moral decline. There will always be some people who believe in an impending apocalypse, but I will show that, as with all other dire predictions, the end is not nigh.

I believe we indeed live in an ethically better world than at any time in the past. How can I possibly believe this, with all the human misery and tragedy surrounding us? It depends on how you define moral improvement. And I define it not by the consequences of people's actions but by what is in people's *hearts*.

More than 100 million deaths were attributed to human conflict in the twentieth century. Does that make the twentieth century the most evil on record? I will argue that there is *less* evil in people's hearts today. Much of the comparison must take into account what I call the three great *amplifiers* that help make today appear more evil:

- The differences in population sizes that distort comparisons between two time periods—for example, when the world had a population of 100 million some 2,500 years ago versus today when the population is fast approaching 7 billion.

- The role of modern weaponry and destructive technology that leverages violence to new heights.

- The role of our always-on global media that make us immediately aware of shameful moral behavior from every corner of the earth.

## Violence Yesterday and Today

The most salient way to gauge moral progress is simply how humans treat other humans. Steven Pinker, a Harvard psychologist, offered much the same argument in his essay, "A History of Violence," wherein he illustrates what is all too clear to me: Today is a much *less* violent period compared to any other epoch in the past. That is true even if we include what I consider a gruesome aberration, the deaths attributable to Fascism, Nazism, and Communism. We may be killing or capable of killing more on an industrial scale, but I aver that the further in the past we go, the more evil was humanity.

Pinker is debunking the mistaken notion that somehow humans are naturally peace-loving prior to being corrupted by modern society. In fact, modernity is associated with much less violence rather than more. "Violence has been in decline over long stretches of history," Pinker writes, "and today we are probably living in the most peaceful moment of our species' time on Earth." History is showing that humans have been getting kinder and gentler over time.

Sam Bowles, an evolutionary biologist, noted that during the last 90,000 years of the Pleistocene Epoch (from about 100,000 years ago until about 10,000 years ago when agriculture emerged), the human population hardly grew. One reason was the extraordinary climatic volatility of the period. But another, Bowles suggests, was that our ancestors were busy killing each other in wars. Working from archaeological records and ethnographic studies, he estimates that wars between different groups could have accounted for a substantial fraction of human deaths—perhaps as much as 15 percent, on average, of those born in any given year.

Social scientists looking back at the empirical evidence see that early societies were much more violent than our own. It is true that raids and battles killed a tiny percentage of the numbers that die in modern warfare, but it affected a much higher percentage of the population. If the wars of the twentieth century had killed the same proportion of the population that died in the wars typical of tribal societies, the casualty rate would have been more like a billion or more deaths rather than 100 million. Certainly that was 100 million too many, but it is clear which is the more humane culture.

James Q. Wilson, in his book *The Moral Sense*, points out that "the greatest and most sustained expansion in the boundaries of the moral sense occurred in the West. Slavery, for example, was common in ancient times and in all parts of the world. It existed among hunter-gatherers and primitive agriculturalists; among many African tribes; among the early Germans and Celts; among some Native Americans; in ancient Greece and Rome; and in China, Japan and the Near East. But it was in the West that slavery was first and most systematically challenged on principled grounds."

People the world over today are much less inclined to resort to violence to resolve conflicts. I also think it is a sign of moral progress when such incidents as Abu Ghraib and My Lai can make people literally sick to their stomachs. In centuries past, these events would not have elicited much condemnation.

## Amplifying Modern Evil

Today's "evil" that we see running across our computer and television screens is really an exponential amplification of the evil that exists in people's hearts. And whatever evil there is, I do not think it is comparable to 500 years ago, much less 5,000 years ago. As I previously discussed, one variable is the enormous difference in population size between then and now. Two other amplifying factors are technology and the media.

Technology leverages the evil of the few in a way that materially affects the lives of the many. In the olden days, it took a thousand evil people to kill a thousand people, mainly by hand-to-hand combat. Today, because of technology, it takes very few evil people to produce a humanitarian disaster. Through the leverage of weapons technology, a few people can become major purveyors of destruction. But more destruction does not mean more evil. I insist that proportionately there are more people in the world today who have love and compassion in their hearts for their fellow human beings, in large part because of religion, than at any time in the past.

The media also play an important role in our evaluation of unfolding events to the point where the world appears to be unraveling, even though it is not. In the olden days before the advent of mass communications, most of man's inhumanity to man was essentially invisible to the vast majority of the world's people; today, much of it becomes instantaneous worldwide news. Most of the cruelty of preceding times was never reported because there was no such thing as the Internet, hundreds of satellite channels, and 24-hour news cycles.

## The Method of Moral Progress

I believe that in the moral realm there is a parallel process to the scientific method; that moral progress proceeds in a manner similar to the way scientific progress takes place. The scientific method allows for the proposal of a hypothesis or theory based on observation. And the key to science is testability, wherein wrong ideas get rejected and correct ideas are retained. We can see a version of the same process occurring in evolution and natural selection—good genetic adaptations that lead to increased fitness are passed on to progeny; bad genetic adaptations just disappear.

I firmly believe that we also have a parallel method taking place, albeit less systematically, in the moral realm. A process of "natural selection" of cultural ideas has been ongoing throughout history. Put most simply, ideas that lead to the greatest *moral* fitness are retained. Depending on the prevailing cultural conditions, those moral ideas that maximize collective benefits and minimize social conflict are preserved. As I already said, this is not systematic, and there are numerous instances when history has taken a wrong turn; but it always seems to self-correct. Bad men and their ideas inevitably fail (Hitler, Stalin). Good men and their ideas invariably succeed (Gandhi, King). This process is similar in the moral sphere to what happens in the scientific sphere with the scientific method. Moral ideas that produce great benefit get passed on to future generations.

## Economic Progress = Moral Progress

For those who acknowledge that we as a civilization have made economic and scientific progress but little or no moral progress, I want to point out that economic and scientific progress *is* moral progress. On the most basic level, economics and science have profound moral implications because they contribute to people's health and physical well-being—a condition not enjoyed by all 6.7 billion people on this planet. Indeed, economic development and its attendant scientific considerations are the foundation of the U.N.'s Millennium Development Goals for the world's poor:

1. Eradicate extreme poverty and hunger.
2. Achieve universal primary education.
3. Promote gender equality and empower women.
4. Reduce child mortality.
5. Improve maternal health.
6. Combat HIV/AIDS, malaria, and other diseases.
7. Ensure environmental sustainability.
8. Develop a global partnership for development.

To the extent that more people in the world are receiving economic and scientific help, we have become a more moral civilization. Lifting people out of poverty is the single most important form of moral progress. Indeed, the very fact that we even choose to consider such global objectives reflects a higher level of moral consciousness. While conditions today remain problematic, it is still a vast improvement over any period in the past.

## Universal Ethic

In one important way, atheists have had a valid criticism of religion. Because each religious tradition is oriented around a conception of one absolute, and because by definition absolutes are incompatible among themselves (there cannot be two supreme realities, much less a hundred), religions may become absolutist, exclusionary, and competitive. But it is in the very nature of these religions to be self-correcting. Unlike the politically sanctioned state, which is founded upon territoriality, religions are founded on the values of peace, compassion, and love.

And over time, we are seeing a growing moral consensus among the world's religions, addressing such issues as intolerance and discrimination, war and peace, abuse of vulnerable populations, freedom of conscience, human rights, and environmental responsibility.

In particular, the one important area where religious and secular people are converging is with respect to their ethical values. A universal ethic is emerging. As James Q. Wilson stated, "The aspiration toward the universal is the chief feature of the moral history of mankind." A growing number of people live under the humanistic ideal of equal respect for all human beings. Americans are familiar with the passage in the Declaration of Independence asserting that "all men are created equal," but they forget how remarkable it is in the history of human relations. And this declaration is becoming more widely espoused and accepted over time. Thus are people increasingly appalled by revelations of torture, human trafficking, ethnic cleansing, global poverty, acts of terrorism, the horrors of war, and the like.

Wilson further writes, "However common the savagery, bloodletting and mendacity of contemporary life, a growing fraction of humankind lives under the claim that men and women are entitled to equal respect. The spread of that claim is extraordinary; even more extraordinary is the fact that so many people sometimes obey it." People have a natural capacity for sympathy, but where once sympathy extended only to those closest to us, today it often encompasses people whom we have never met. Wilson concurs: "The most remarkable change in the moral history of mankind has been the rise—and occasionally the application—of the view that all people, and not just one's own kind, are entitled to fair treatment." If that is not moral progress, then I do not know what is. And as I have been emphasizing, a big part of this moral universalism derives from religion.

Though their paths are diverse, all major religious traditions posit one reality of transcendent value, possessing the attributes of compassion, wisdom, and love, in conscious relation to which humans can find their proper fulfillment. And so a universal ethic is emerging that is at once religious and humanistic. Today, more than anything, religions are dedicated to alleviating human suffering and advancing human well-being. Throughout history, religion has served to enhance the cohesiveness of groups and foster cooperation within groups, although that frequently meant conflict with outside groups. More recently, religion has been devoted to harmonizing different groups as well as encouraging wider affinities and global-scale cooperation.

So I think it is important to distinguish between old-time religion and modern religion. Whether liberal or conservative, religion today emphasizes salvation not only of true believers but of all of humanity. Therefore what Morris Ginsberg wrote in 1947 is even more true in the twenty-first century: "A list of virtues or duties drawn up by a Buddhist would not differ greatly from one drawn up by a Christian, a Confucianist, a Muhammedan or a Jew. All ethico-religious systems are universalist in scope."

The religious-secular convergence taking place is specifically focused on *humanism*. This was exemplified recently in the speech Pope Benedict XVI gave to the United Nations on the sixtieth anniversary of the "Universal Declaration of Human Rights." Pope Benedict's focus was on the "universality, indivisibility and interdependence of human rights" in international affairs, wherein "the promotion of human rights remains the most effective strategy for eliminating inequalities between countries and social groups, and for increasing security." He referred several times to the "dignity of every human person" and "the unity of the human family" as he emphasized the imperative "to place the human person at the heart of institutions, laws and the workings of society." The pope further stated that "human rights are increasingly being presented as the common language and ethical substratum of international relations" and that "recognition of the transcendent value of every man and woman favors conversion of heart, which then leads to a commitment to resist violence, terrorism and war, and promote peace and justice."

Compare those thoughts with the following statement I adapted from the "Humanist Manifesto" of the American Humanist Association, which could have come from any progressive religious leader:

> *Humanism is a secular philosophy that affirms our ability and responsibility to lead ethical lives of personal fulfillment that aspire to the greater good of humanity. Humanists are concerned for the well-being of all, are committed to diversity, and respect those of differing yet humane views. We work to uphold the equal enjoyment of human rights and civil liberties in an open society. Thus engaged in the flow of life, we aspire to this vision with the informed conviction that humanity has the ability to progress toward its highest ideals. We are committed to treating each person as having inherent worth and dignity, and to making informed choices in a context of freedom consonant with responsibility.*

## Conclusion

Increasingly the days are past when religions could serve humanity by championing a single culture or civilization to the exclusion of others. In a growing universal ethic, religious leaders are emphasizing a fundamental consensus on core values and ethical affirmations that they hold in common. And that is exactly the mission behind the Tony Blair Faith Foundation, established by the former British prime minister.

Blair's initiative is distinctive because it goes one step further than the typical commitment to inter-faith dialogue. He wants to use the power of faith to help address some of the world's most pressing social and geopolitical problems. Thus he states, "You cannot understand the modern world unless you understand the importance of religious faith. Faith motivates, galvanizes, organizes and integrates millions upon millions of people." According to Blair, faith provides a common basis for values and beliefs that enable people to cooperate for the common good. "Faith is part of our future, and the values it brings with it are an essential part of making globalization work."

# Religion, Fundamentalism, and Violence

The question to be asked is not why religion becomes violent, but why people resort to collective violence at all. Much of this violence may appear to be religious in nature, but the reality of fundamentalist behavior is actually a complex interplay among individual psychology, group dynamics, and a mixture of cultural and political forces. In truth, radical elements can exist in any ideological group; religion by itself plays a relatively modest role in the fundamentalism process.

The militant atheists lament that religion is the foremost source of the world's violence is contradicted by three realities: Most religious organizations do not foster violence; many nonreligious groups do engage in violence; and many religious moral precepts encourage nonviolence. Indeed, we can confidently assert that if religion was the sole or primary force behind wars, then secular ideologies should be relatively benign by comparison, which history teaches us has not been the case. Revealingly, in his *Encyclopedia of Wars*, Charles Phillips chronicled a total of 1,763 conflicts throughout history, of which just 123 were categorized as religious. And it is important to note further that over the last century the most brutality has been perpetrated by nonreligious cult figures (Hitler, Stalin, Kim Jong-Il, Mao Zedong, Saddam Hussein, Pol Pot, Idi Amin, Fidel Castro, Slobodan Milosevic, Robert Mugabe—you get the picture). Thus to attribute the impetus behind violence mainly to religious sentiments is a highly simplistic interpretation of history.

The purpose of this chapter is to examine the central radicalizing forces that contribute to collective violence and fundamentalist behavior of all types. While this chapter is not meant to be an all-encompassing study, it will clearly show that religion is just one of many factors in a highly complex process.

## Organizational Dynamics and the Sources of Group Conflict

The need for group affiliation and identity is an integral part of what it means to be human. Early in my life I witnessed our susceptibility to group dynamics in the mass idolatry exhibited at rock concerts. Indeed, one need go no further than a political rally, a World Cup soccer match, or an antiwar protest march to see how powerful group processes can be.

### There's Identity in Numbers

Group affiliation is often criticized by sociological observers who see it as a violation of one's individuality and authenticity. But rather than surrendering our true selves, involvement in a group context paradoxically helps to constitute that very self. The problem is when those group affiliations become extremist affairs.

Arthur Koestler had some penetrating words to say about the dangers inherent in extremist group behavior:

> The continuous disasters in history are mainly due to an
> excessive capacity and urge to become identified with a
> tribe, nation, church or cause, and to espouse its credo

*uncritically and enthusiastically …. No historian would
deny that the part played by crimes committed for personal
motives are quantitatively negligible compared to those
committed out of the self-transcending devotion to a flag,
leader, religious faith or political conviction.*

As Koestler is noting, there is a huge difference between individually motivated violence, typically an expression of assertive and defensive tendencies, and collective violence, which is most frequently an expression of self-transcending and group-identification impulses.

In the modern world, major conflicts are based on four modes of collective affiliation: religious, nationalist, ethnic, and socioeconomic. Further, each instance of group conflict is structured as an in-group/out-group dynamic: the individual has a positive relationship with the in-group (affiliation, obedience, conformity) and a negative relationship with the out-group (differentiation, discrimination, opposition). This polarization is accentuated by the individual member's isolation from outsiders and total submersion in group ideology.

Individuals in cohesive groups do not exhibit a personal conscience. Rather, they have a collective center of gravity where some higher purpose becomes the driving force for unity and action. Often group identity becomes more important than one's individual autonomy. This is vividly expressed by a soldier's experience in battle. Philip Caputo writes in *A Rumor of War:* "I have attempted to describe the intimacy of life in infantry battalions, where the communion between men is as profound as any between lovers. Actually it is more so … devotion, simple and selfless, the sentiment of belonging to each other."

The influence of group identity on extremist behavior is often underestimated. Regarding Islamic terrorism, for example, the majority of casual observers attribute participation in jihadist movements to *aversive* factors such as the Palestinian-Israeli conflict, America's presence in Islamic countries, economic deprivation, and disaffection with government leaders—when it is *attractive* factors within the group that are actually more influential in bringing together and convincing members.

Scott Atran, an academic, and Marc Sageman, a former CIA operative, found that the biggest determinant of which people go on to become terrorists from among millions of potential warriors is group dynamics rather than religious, economic, or societal factors. They found that some 90 percent of terrorists were influenced by friendship and/or kinship in joining groups through which they derived a powerful sense of belonging and purpose. Indeed, for such terror-group members, often community is more important than ideology in the radicalizing process. And frequently the commitment of individual members can become so passionate that group goals justify almost any means, including violence.

Extremist groups are transformative to the point that, paradoxically, while individual group members tend to be clinically "normal" people, the *group* exhibits psychotic behavior. This explains a surprising phenomenon: psychologists tell us that suicide bombers and other terrorists generally have unremarkable personalities. One observer cited in Walter Reich's *The Origins of Terrorism* stated, "The outstanding common characteristic of terrorists is their normality." Another observer wrote, "The best documented generalization is that terrorists do not show any striking psychopathology." Yet terrorist groups are capable of the most heinous and horrific acts. Once together, group members tend to radicalize each other, the more strident leading the way, to the point where even martyrdom can become a symbol of success within a group context. In one such instance, a 25-year-old Jordanian jihadist who had yet to die in combat lamented to a *New York Times* reporter that his martyred friends are the lucky ones.

## The Political Corruption of Religion

Large-scale group conflicts are rarely about only one form of affiliation. Nazism, for example, was a combination of ethnic, nationalist, and political-social forms of group affiliation; religion technically played a minor role. Indeed, for more than two centuries from the American and French revolutions to the end of the Cold War, major conflicts had little to do with religion. Thus, to single out religious organizations for their political failings is unfair. In one amazing example, the former Yugoslavia has disintegrated into seven different countries, with economic conditions and ethno-nationalism playing a much bigger role than religion.

The more combustible religious conflicts emerge when other forms of group affiliation are involved, such as ethnic identification, state and economic interests, and nationalistic ambitions. I call this the *political corruption* of religion, where religion is essentially subordinated to nonreligious objectives. Usually cultural observers unfairly emphasize religion's contribution to these conflicts, while downplaying the political dimension. For example, religious differences are certainly part of the Israeli-Palestinian conflict, but the conflict is kept red-hot largely by nationalist and tribal-ethnic considerations. Further, sectarian conflicts in Nigeria (between Muslims and Christians) and India (between Hindi and Muslims) have been potentiated by tribalism and nationalism. If you need more proof that the political often takes precedence over the religious: All over the world a number of Islamic radicals are cooperating with Godless communists to work against their common secular enemies in the West. And it has been reported that in Beirut's southern suburbs, portraits of Hugo Chavez hang alongside pictures of Hezbollah leader Hassan Nasrallah.

All this goes to show that dogma is not the exclusive province of religion, and secular political movements are just as destructive as religious ideologies. Every belief system has its hardened acolytes and its sectarian divisions. And it is clear that most modern examples of collective violence (such as between Serbs and Croats of former Yugo-slavia; Hutu and Tutsi of Rwanda; Fatah and Hamas in Palestine) have had little to do with religion per se. In still another example, the Suda-nese war in Darfur is considered more about ethnic and tribal tensions than religious identification. And Muslim citizens rioted in France but not in the United States, suggesting that the tensions had more to do with social discrimination and economic integration than religion.

Further, the recent Tibetan convulsions in China were not about Buddhism, but were essentially an expression of a nationalist and eth-nic liberation movement. This 60-year-old conflict is largely secular in nature. While the atheistic Chinese government is well known for its persecution of religious groups, it is not because China considers religion evil, but because religion is one organized ideology among oth-ers it considers competitive with the ruling communist party. Indeed, China's nationalistic paranoia was recently on display when it banned Buddhist monks in Tibet from reincarnating without government per-mission. The real purpose of this decree is purely political: It prevents the Dalai Lama from being succeeded by someone outside China.

## The Fundamentalist Personality

After World War II, a group of scholars developed the idea of a par-ticular personality type to help explain the Holocaust and racial/ethnic hatred. Among other insights, the authors noted this individual's incli-nation to "submit blindly to power and authority"—hence the title of their now-classic study, *The Authoritarian Personality*.

I want to revise this theory for the contemporary world of collective violence. Contrary to what many believe, it was not primarily religious faith that inspired 10 Islamists to navigate two jets into New York's World Trade Center, but a particular psychosocial type that I call the fundamentalist personality that applied to these men (note: they are most frequently men), but which did not apply to the tens of millions of other people exposed to the same religious and sociopolitical forces.

Please note: I am not a scientist or scholar. My theory of the fundamentalist personality is more personal impression than social science. But I believe the concept goes a long way to explain how seemingly ordinary people initiate or participate in group violence, and why only certain people adopt extremist ideologies or exert an extremist influence within otherwise moderate groups. And I emphasize *group*—because none of these behaviors is conceivable outside of a group context or collective movement.

When we think of fundamentalism, religious fundamentalism immediately comes to mind. The term was first used by conservative Protestants in the nineteenth century who wanted to reemphasize the "fundamentals" of the Christian tradition. And well-respected books by Karen Armstrong (*The Battle for God*), Martin E. Marty (*Fundamentalism Observed*), and Malise Ruthven (*Fundamentalism*) have interpreted the issue entirely in religious terms. But that is unfortunate, because fundamentalism broadly defined can be found in all kinds of group affiliations, collective behavior, and belief systems. Fundamentalism is certainly not an exclusively religious phenomenon; secular fundamentalists must also be acknowledged.

Within every belief system or political movement, individual members exist on a continuum that ranges from pragmatic accommodation to uncompromising fanaticism, where some group members are more easily inclined to extremist behavior than others. I want to explain the characteristics that differentiate the extremist or fundamentalist personality from the majority of people who, despite similar experiences of oppression and victimization, are not radicalized and merely seek to live and let live.

The more we analyze belief systems of any kind, the more we understand that certain individuals are specifically attracted to extremist groups and are prepared to help radicalize any ideology. And religion is just one factor among many in the development of the fundamentalist personality. Indeed, fundamentalism doesn't have to be of a religious nature—any secular ideology will do.

So if you happen upon a Christian extremist—one who holds steadfastly to his belief, brooks no challenge, and is excessively critical of competing creeds—it is a good bet that person was not made a fundamentalist by his religion. Rather, a number of genetic, experiential, and sociopolitical factors conspire to make a fundamentalist, especially one who is inclined toward collective aggression.

## Messianic Missionaries

The most prominent feature of the fundamentalist is his involvement in a messianic movement. Messianism is hardly the exclusive province of religion. Messianic belief systems can be of a religious nature, but they exist within every type of ideological context, including such recent secular examples as the political radicalism of Marxism-Leninism; the utopian fascisms of Europe; the nationalistic ambitions of the Irish Republican Army; the separatist goals of the Basque terror group ETA; the anarchic visions of the Weather Underground; the cosmic fantasies of Heaven's Gate; the maniacal insurgency of the Khmer Rouge; and the scientific salvation offered by the most fervent strain of atheism.

Members of messianic groups exhibit a higher-than-average propensity to surrender their freedom and individuality to a collective identity and characteristically exhibit polarizing, us-versus-them thinking. The more extreme members thrive on conspiracy theories, xenophobia, moral superiority, and an apocalyptic vision of good versus evil. Fundamentalist group members typically lack critical judgment; abhor complexity and ambiguity; and divide the world into strict, sharply delineated categories. Easily outraged and aggrieved, they see themselves as victims of powerful forces against which they must fight. They see the current world order as radically unjust and in need of overthrow, using violence if necessary. Fundamentalist groups do not have opponents or challengers; they have enemies to demonize and dehumanize. Ideological "moderates" are seen as appeasers and traitors.

Fundamentalists are often recognized by their single-minded obedience to charismatic leaders, an inerrant interpretation of "sacred" beliefs and myths, and the use of violent methods for idealistic goals (e.g., setting fire to an abortion clinic; bombing a government building; committing mass suicide). In their conception, all that benefits the group represents the universal good; all that threatens the group becomes evil. I would borrow Robert Lifton's concept of "totalism," where a particular ideology makes up the entirety of their worldview.

The dominant emotion in the fundamentalist personality is dread. Rather than allowing themselves to be gradually transformed through an open encounter with their ideological opponents, extremists fear that any compromise will invariably lead to a dismantling of their life's purpose and certainty—hence their drive to defend their beliefs at all costs. Violence and terror are, in their mind, pure acts of self-defense.

I am continually amazed by small groups of fundamentalist people who engage in magical thinking and believe they can rally the silent majority to their particular mission of saving the world. The world is a pretty big place. Yet these delusions of grandeur persist. For example, the contemporary version of Students for a Democratic Society (SDS) has only 3,000 members among the nation's 15 million college students— just 1 in 5,000. One SDS activist interviewed in *The New York Times* said that his goal is to "change the world." He and his colleagues are focused on persuading masses of people to join them. "It's about getting 50, 60, 100 million people together to take action," he says, despite the obvious odds against him and his brethren.

Then there's the activity of Chelsea Gerlach and the other 20 or so members of "the Family," a radical faction of the environmental activist group Earth Liberation Front (ELF). She received a nine-year prison sentence for her role in committing arson in the name of "saving the earth." The Family's revolutionary intent was to hasten the collapse of the "ecocidal empire," as members referred to America. From 1996 to 2001, the Family was responsible for at least 15 fires across the western United States, which they referred to as a "cleansing force." One ELF supporter was clear about the ends justifying the means and equating arson with civil disobedience: "I would go back to the Boston Tea Party and the American Revolution. Sometimes you have to break government law."

This is characteristic thinking among extremists of all stripes, including those who are the most destructive—terrorists. There are probably no more than 50,000 terrorists willing to commit mass murder of innocents organized in small isolated cadres around the globe. Despite obvious limitations, violent fanatics believe that through a scattering of isolated terrorist acts they can permanently alter the global political, cultural, and religious landscape.

## Radicalization within the Group

We are all aware that many cultlike groups try to indoctrinate new members to become true believers. Less well known is the self-selected radicalization process that often takes place among fundamentalist types. Intolerant or embittered people naturally gravitate to causes and splinter groups that give expression to their extremist tendencies, which in turn reinforces the intolerant inclinations of the individual and the group.

Recent research cited by Cass Sunstein, for example, has shown that people with a particular political orientation who join a like-minded group emerge from that group with stronger political leanings than they started with. "In almost every group," Sunstein writes, "people ended up with more extreme positions …. The result is group polarization, which occurs when like-minded people interact and end up in a more extreme position in line with their original inclinations." And with the Internet added to the fundamentalist equation, it is now easier than ever for extremists of all types to find their ideological soul mates and reinforce their radical thinking.

This process is very similar to what Irving Janis described as "groupthink," whose characteristics include illusions of invulnerability; presumptions of group righteousness; one-dimensional perception of the enemy as evil; intolerance of challenges to the group's beliefs; and the suppression of critical thinking. In groupthink, these characteristics reinforce one another and result in an intensification of group beliefs, prejudices, and objectives.

It thus becomes clear that in the case of religious extremists, it is not so much religion that breeds intolerance, but the intolerant who embrace a certain interpretation of religion—and who likely become more intolerant through group involvement. For example, does anyone really think that the elimination of religious faith will put an end to such extremists as Osama bin Laden? The bin Laden family is enormous (the patriarch had 22 wives and 54 children), but only Osama became overtly radicalized.

That violent people often cite passages from religious texts as justification is not an indictment of those religious texts. For these people, the Bible or Koran serves as a Rorschach inkblot; they invariably find whatever they are looking for. Every great civilization has incorporated theology into its politics as a way to sanctify its laws and leadership. Every messianic cult—from the Branch Davidians and People's Temple in America to the Aum Shinrikyo of Japan to the Muslim Brotherhood and al Qaeda in the Islamic world—borrows the apocalyptic language and imagery of religious texts. But that does not make those texts or those religions responsible.

Indeed, experts who study extreme violent behavior such as suicide bombings are increasingly skeptical about religion's role. Marc Sageman argues in his book, *Leaderless Jihad*—which is based on a study of 500 jihadists who used violence against the United States and its allies— that the majority of young men who joined terrorist groups knew very little about Islam and grew up in secular homes. Their use of religion to justify violence should not blind analysts to the primacy of personality and sociological factors in the radicalizing process (including the belief among self-annihilators that their peer group will see them as heroes).

## Enduring Personality Traits

Studies with twins have shown that individual political persuasions have a substantial genetic component. For example, identical twins are more likely to give the same answers to political questions than nonidentical twins. Scientists have also shown that liberals and conservatives have different patterns of brain activity. Related to that, a decades-long study has found that personality traits associated with liberalism or conservatism later in life actually show up in preschoolers. While there are no specific genes that code for one's perspective on gay rights or American foreign policy, for example, it is well known that certain genes shape enduring personality or temperamental qualities, which can influence political opinions.

Based on these insights, I am betting that fundamentalism is also significantly influenced by personality traits, genetic factors, and brain chemistry. But I do not think scientists are looking at all the correct correlations when investigating political orientation. They are seeking, for example, the personality distinctions between liberals and conservatives. What they are missing, however, are the commonalities between extremist liberals and extremist conservatives—two political types that have fundamentalism in common.

We are thus acknowledging that fundamentalists can be of either a right-wing or left-wing variety. And they all exhibit both reactionary and radical traits: cleaving to fundamental principles at the same time they are committed to changing the existing culture to conform to those fundamentals. They claim to want to "change the world," but they actually detest change so much that they adamantly cling to an uncompromising ideal of how the world should be. Liberal fundamentalists are little different from their conservative counterparts, exhibiting an unerring and intolerant commitment to their own ideas—creating the paradox of a closed-minded liberal.

But perhaps the allure of extremism is as simple as the fact that it frequently leads to a high incidence of life satisfaction. Arthur Brooks, who has done considerable research into the personal factors correlated with Americans' happiness, has found that extremists on both sides of the political spectrum are happier than moderates. Some 35 percent of those who call themselves "extremely liberal" say they are very happy, against only 22 percent of ordinary liberals. For conservatives, the gap is 48 percent to 43 percent. Extremists are happier, Brooks conjectures, because they are more certain about their righteousness. The problem, as we have seen, is that this attitude often leads extremists to conclude that the other side is not merely wrong, but evil.

## External Radicalizing Forces

In addition to a number of personality and group-dynamic factors, underlying social and political conditions also contribute to the alienation and radicalization that result in fundamentalist behavior. This is especially true in the volatile Middle East. While many observers like to blame the West for the victimization and humiliation they claim engenders Islamic group violence, I lay the problem squarely on the authoritarian nature of Islamic government and culture. The lack of democratic traditions in this part of the world is the biggest enabler of group violence. It is in repressive, autocratic sociopolitical environments that the fundamentalist personality is able to find its most lethal modes of expression.

While prospective fundamentalists are found everywhere, I am a strong believer that certain political institutions and forms of social organization can potentiate or mitigate fundamentalist inclinations.

## Democracy Is an Essential Part of the Solution

There is no doubt in my mind that an open political and economic system is a prerequisite for a society free from all kinds of collective violence, including that of a religious nature. It is not a coincidence that Christianity in the West emerged as a tolerant theology respectful of individual liberties at about the same time that democratic principles became widespread. Further, history teaches us that no two democracies have ever been at war with each other. A democracy is where a "wisdom of crowds" phenomenon takes place. More than any other form of social organization, democracy encourages peace among its citizens and within the global community. Specifically, democracy counters extremist fundamentalism within its own midst in five interrelated ways.

### Political Recourse

Most important, democracy provides a legitimate political outlet for grievances without resorting to violence. American-style democracy in particular allows for conflict resolution that is not possible in an autocratic society; it allows for integration into the political system rather than alienation and exclusion.

A government that mistreats its citizens and fosters a culture of cruelty (for example, in parts of the world where women are stoned to death under Shariah law) is like abusive parents who teach their children that violence is an acceptable way to resolve problems. In a liberal democracy, people learn methods of conflict resolution that respect all participants.

## Separation of Church and State

I would argue that the bigotry, chauvinism, and intolerance of religious fundamentalism are not a justification for atheism. Rather, they're an argument for the separation of church and state. The unholy alliance of religion and politics is a combustible formula for messianic crusades. Western democracy makes a strenuous effort to separate religion from politics. By keeping religion away from the instruments of the state and political calculation divorced from religious devotions, collective violence is minimized. In European history, kings interfered in the affairs of popes and priests far too often, and vice versa, with frequently disastrous consequences. Yet history also teaches us that to the extent that religion becomes fully differentiated from the state, religious institutions often become a positive force for peace and reconciliation.

The potential lethal effects of combining religion and politics were clearly illustrated in a recent *New York Times* photograph: A masked militiaman in Baghdad is shown carrying both a rocket launcher and a Koran during a parade by the Mahdi Army. It is interesting to ask: Is this a religious scholar carrying a gun? Or is this a political soldier carrying a Koran? I submit that it really does not matter whether religion is injected into politics (such as in Iran) or religion is infected by politics (such as in Saudi Arabia); politics and religion make for an inflammatory combination.

Osama bin Laden's horrific atrocities were never primarily motivated by religion. He sought a fatwa from a deviant cleric to justify the killing of innocents in the eyes of believers. This is politics, not religion. The answer is not to renounce religious faith, but to keep religion out of politics. Note that I am not suggesting that religious *individuals* stay out of politics, but that religious *institutions* stay out of politics. We are all individuals who are free to vote our conscience and values. And those values may in fact be informed and influenced by our religious beliefs, which in turn affect our political choices. But when religious groups become politically motivated (or vice versa), this can easily lead to competitiveness over power and authority.

As historian Mark Lilla observed, it was when a polity centered on God was replaced with a liberal-democratic system centered on man that the West moved permanently away from wars of religion. Thus in the United States we have so little religiously inspired violence because we keep church and state separate. On virtually every point of contention between secular liberalism and religious traditionalism, mainline American culture chooses the secular side.

This practice means subordinating the demands of religious groups to secular laws and values whenever the religious and the secular collide in the public square. But this is far different from state-forced secularization with the concomitant marginalization of religion, as is implied by bans against Muslim women wearing headscarves in Turkey or France. The suppression of religious practice by the state can have the deleterious effect of driving religion underground, where surreptitious radicalization can more easily take place.

### Living on More Than Religion Alone

It is unfortunate that in many parts of the world, especially in much of the Islamic world, a person has little more than his religion on which to base his self-esteem. That may have been workable or even desirable in the early days of civilization, but in the tumultuous modern world where a plethora of potentially conflicting ideas, mores, cultures, and people cross porous borders, a person needs to rely on many sources for his sense of purpose and communal validation. This is not to diminish the enduring value of religion, but it is an acknowledgement that for most people in the modern world, religion is often not enough.

What we see clearly is that in a political environment where most personal choices are restricted and people have only their religion, when those religious ideas are challenged (as they almost always are in our interdependent global age), it is invariably experienced as an existential threat. Under those conditions, the recourse to violence is often seen as an act of self-preservation.

Only a liberal democracy offers numerous secular choices for the affirmation of self-esteem as a kind of psychological "diversification of risk." People need more than one source, whatever that may be, upon which to base their personal validation.

## Conflict Sublimation

For people who develop a fundamentalist orientation even within a pluralistic society, democracy offers many opportunities for the sublimation of extremist tendencies into culturally acceptable modes of expression. Indeed, I believe that in America we are surrounded by millions of what I call "benign fanatics" and "free radicals." But instead of resorting to collective violence, I am convinced that most such people express their extremist inclinations through socially sanctioned forms of intense competition and counterculture opposition, where people can experience all the drama of an Armageddon-like battle in such areas as business, sports, politics, and culture.

Anyone who has ever been to a Yankees-Red Sox game, been an employee of Microsoft or Google, been a member of a union or political party, or joined a pro-life or pro-choice group has seen the manifestation of a relatively harmless form of cultlike behavior every bit as fervent as the sort practiced within ideologically motivated mass movements. We may lament the "culture wars" that many of these group affiliations engender, but most of these people physically harm no one and contribute to America's ongoing cultural discourse.

## Freedom of Religion

It seems ironic that allowing for freedom of religion results in less religious radicalism rather than more. But that is precisely what the U.S. Constitution's First Amendment provides for in admonishing that "Congress shall make no law respecting the establishment of religion or prohibiting the free exercise thereof." This became the great engine of American religiosity, creating a new system where membership in a church was purely a voluntary act.

The free market for religion allows for a competitive religious environment that precludes the dominance of any one tradition and allows for considerable religious diversity. In America, God is not dead; he just comes in more varieties. A recent Pew study of 35,000 adults revealed that as America remains a vigorously religious country, its religious marketplace is extraordinarily competitive and dynamic. While 78 percent of Americans say they belong to the Christian tradition in one of its manifestations, more than one in four adults (28 percent) have swapped a religious tradition in which they were raised for another. And nearly four in ten (37 percent) of married Americans have a spouse with a different religious affiliation. As *The Economist* pointed out, a major reason for this dynamism is that in America, churches compete for new members in much the same way companies compete for customers.

This tradition strikes much of the world as incomprehensible, but it makes for an optimal combination of religious expression and tolerance. More important, a democratic system engenders religious innovation that is focused on the *consumers* of religion. The result is not a religion whose survival depends on the promotion of a static orthodoxy, but a religion that is much more market-responsive—that is, humane and empathetic. Saudi Arabia enforces religious orthodoxy with police and prisons. History has shown that this can only result in an authoritarian religion obsessed with its own power.

## Hypothetical Example

Imagine, if you will, the son of a Palestinian fruit grower who is educated in Hamas-dominated territory, where as a child he learns about hatred for Jews and Christians. Day after day he sees the injustices imposed on Palestinian people as presented by the highly politicized television networks Al Aksa (Hamas) and Al Manar (Hezbollah). He hears imams offering sermons and prayers supposedly derived from the Koran that preach political struggle. He is also outraged by the Danish cartoon caricatures of the Prophet. He is exposed to conspiracy theories such as the Protocols of the Elders of Zion as truth. He believes that the West is perpetrating a war against Islam. And he lives in a political environment defined by corruption, unemployment, and state despotism. Imagine further that this person, who now carries around with him a festering anger and smoldering resentment, comes under the influence of a mosque offering radical solutions and martyrdom—where largely political goals are cloaked in religious language. That person may in time turn to political violence.

In America, this person's typical circumstances would be very different. Such a person, first of all, would rarely be as radicalized in the United States. As explained previously, many mitigating factors and moderating forces are likely to result in a person who does not feel quite so victimized and alienated. But even if a man grows up to be culturally outraged, he has many channels available to him through which to express his dissent in relatively peaceful and productive ways. Depending on the particular issue, he could protest in front of the United Nations, mobilize like-minded people, join a reformist movement, vote for a political candidate, or even become a well-paid lobbyist. He could also publish newspaper articles or create a dedicated website to inform the world.

The point is, within a pluralistic democracy, rarely is there a need for political or religious violence. On the other hand, in the autocratic Middle East, where theology and politics mix easily, where religion is the only source of a person's self-worth, where free expression is suppressed, and where opportunity for economic and social progress is restricted—violence is often seen as a viable option for social and political change.

## Competing in the Marketplace of Ideas

In a long-ago period in history, people existed in theologically and culturally self-contained tribes and villages dominated by one absolutist version of the truth. The indigenous belief systems of such societies were largely closed and rarely challenged. But that was to change dramatically as these self-enclosed territories began to interrelate on a grand scale.

Increasing cultural and economic interconnectedness resulted in the inconvenient revelation that other people also had gods and truths—and they were different. The problem with absolutist beliefs is their inherent incompatibility with other absolutist beliefs. I call this the Law of Absolutes: Like two physical objects that cannot occupy the same space at the same time, two absolute beliefs cannot occupy the same *mind* at the same time.

The institutionalized establishment within each closed society has tried at various times to protect their indigenous beliefs from outside influences, but could not do so indefinitely. Their borders—geographic, economic, and ideological—grew increasingly porous. The inevitable result has been a competitive ideological and spiritual marketplace where wars have had one thing in common: They were fought for a way of living, a way of believing.

Most of the West has evolved beyond being self-contained and inward-looking societies through the proliferation of many global institutions: media and communications, travel and immigration, economic and financial interdependence, international consumer culture, multinational corporations, and education and entertainment. We in the West have come to accept that a mixture of customs, beliefs, fashions, and values is not only normal, it is frequently desirable.

That is not true for much of the rest of the world. The forces of globalization and the broadening of minds they require are still being fiercely resisted by cultures that seek to remain closed—which is essentially impossible at this time in history. Hence the ongoing clash of ideologies and the extremists who champion them.

## Open and Closed Religion

The crucial issue in the fundamentalist equation is whether a religion is open or closed. And this can only really be understood in terms of whether the sponsoring society is open (democratic and pluralistic) or closed (authoritarian and defensive).

An open system is self-criticizing, self-correcting, and self-purging; it allows for progress and compromise. That is why in America the lunatic fringe stays on the fringe. (It's no coincidence that former Klansman David Duke was a featured speaker at an Iranian conference denying the Holocaust; his views do not have much currency in the United States.) That's also why in America good ideas that originally were outside the mainstream (such as abolition, civil rights, and women's rights) have been adopted by the mainstream. While totalitarian societies persecute and silence religious innovators, an open religion accommodates, and even invites, dissent. Multiple religious creeds can coexist, but with the qualification that only *moderate* belief systems can live in harmony with other moderate beliefs.

What makes for religious innovation is an open society that properly mediates the competitive marketplace of ideas. The "creative disruption" of an open society fosters moral progress in religion; it results in a religion that evolves and grows with (rather than against) science and history. An open religious system such as that in the United States leads to greater diversity and tolerance. It teaches that all people share in the worth and dignity conferred by God, including people holding competing religious beliefs.

This tolerance was made evident in a recent study from the Pew Forum on Religion and Public Life. In it, although a majority of Americans say religion is very important to them, nearly three-quarters (70 percent) say that many beliefs besides their own can lead to salvation. The report, the "U.S. Religious Landscape Survey," reveals a broad trend toward tolerance and an ability among many Americans to accommodate beliefs that might contradict the doctrines of their professed faiths.

It used to be that all worldly activity was permeated with the divine. Religion defined every role and every rule. That would still be fine in a closed society. But a closed religion in an open, global society is a contradiction that cannot persist indefinitely. Information in today's world is so diffuse that a closed religion will invariably be challenged again and again. For a religion confronting change, the only alternatives to innovation are to become moribund (as in much of Europe) or seek to destroy competitors (as in much of Islam). In the former category, religion becomes a static institution, which is reflected in the fact that an American is four times likelier than a Frenchman to attend a house of worship regularly, and eight times more likely than a Norwegian. In the latter category, a religion can easily be corrupted by an authoritarian sociopolitical climate wherein that religion comes to express several dangerous tendencies: an absolutist claim to truth; blind obedience to leaders; and a righteous, end-justifies-the-means mentality.

In the case of militant Islam, we are witnessing a defensive reaction against the very nature of the modern world—freedom and its concomitant characteristics of tolerance, pluralism, accommodation, and diversity. Erich Fromm long ago identified the tendency among many people to escape the responsibilities, ambiguity, and contradictions inherent in freedom. When this happens, ideological totalism is often the preferred option.

A democratic society is not a guarantee of an open, healthy-minded religion, but such a religion certainly cannot flourish in an authoritarian society. When repressive Arab governments, like Egypt, lock opposition parties such as the Muslim Brotherhood out of power, they push pious people toward the extremes. For all its flaws, Western religion has bequeathed a tolerance of diverse views within an overarching rational framework supported by a robust moral paradigm that offers the best guarantor of human freedom and dignity. As Sir Jonathan Sachs, chief rabbi of the British Commonwealth, reminds us, "Those who are confident of their faith are not threatened but enlarged by the different faiths of others."

## The Future of Islamic Fundamentalism

A large portion of the Muslim world is a failure—not as a self-contained culture, but within our global and pluralistic world. More than any other modern religious tradition, much of Islam just does not get along with others; its convulsions reflect its difficulty integrating into the modern world and absorbing the kind of challenges to which all religions are today subjected.

For example, the reaction among many Muslims to critiques of Islam—Theo van Gogh's film, *Submission*; the Danish cartoons satirizing Muhammad; Salman Rushdie's *The Satanic Verses*; and the Dutch parliamentarian Geert Wilders' film about the Koran, *Fitna*—has been calls for their creators' death (accomplished in the case of Mr. van Gogh). The Western world long ago learned to train a skeptical eye on religion. The Islamic world is currently not amenable to such discourse.

However, I predict that in time Islam will open up to change. I believe that Islam is on the same trajectory as Christianity before it, and I expect that Islamic fundamentalism will evolve to be more like its Western counterpart, where collective violence is rare. But this will only happen as democracy, open societies, and plurality take hold. Participatory democracy is by far humanity's best political system to achieve a sustainable compromise among myriad conflicting ideologies. I firmly believe that some version of democracy, with its emphasis on human rights, is a natural birthright. I do not believe there are cultural "exceptions" to democratic aspirations, although there may be cultural differences in how democracy can best be realized in a particular society.

Muslims want a better life as much as anyone else. And if we look closely, we can see that a growing number of moderate Muslims are beginning to publicly reject the nihilism, bigotry, and intolerance of fundamentalist Islam. This message was reinforced by the late Benazir Bhutto in her book *Reconciliation:*

> It is my firm belief that until Muslims revert to the traditional interpretation of Islam—in which "you shall have your religion and I shall have mine" is respected and adhered to—the factional strife within Muslim countries will continue. Those who teach the killing of adherents of other sects or religions are damaging Muslim societies.

## The Enduring Value of Religious Identity

Utopian-minded observers for centuries have put forward the idea of a worldwide community of people and nations as a rational culmination of human history. But people will always need tribal affiliations along nationalistic, ethnic, racial, political, economic, and religious lines.

One of the reasons religious allegiance persists is because it offers a distinctive type of group identification. The implication: Whatever collective identity that might be lost by the hypothetical elimination of religion of necessity would be made up by other forms of group affiliation. And as history has taught, secular groups are no less conflict-ridden than religious groups. Indeed, without religion's self-correcting emphasis on ethical principles and compassionate behavior, the situation could be far worse.

It is a paradox of the modern age that global integration has not led to a weakening of group identity, but rather to a strengthening of nationalist and ethnic allegiances. This reflects the sociological fact that we all need to be *a part of* something larger than ourselves and, at the same time, *apart from* other selves. We assert our differences more fiercely precisely because we are less and less different from one another.

The most we can hope for is not a world free of divisions, but rather a world where people aligned with one group or another do not resort to collective aggression. We want to affirm diversity and plurality, but do away with violent conflict. And within that scenario, I assert that religion has an overwhelmingly positive role to play. We need a universalism that respects everyone's inherent right to human dignity, regardless of group affiliation.

I believe that as a global community we are moving toward a greater acceptance of human universals. As Reinhold Niebuhr wrote, "Men seek a universal standard of human good." And religion remains best positioned to provide those universal values.

# The Spectrum of Religiosity

Our culture's previous attempts to discuss God and religion have treated the subject as if it were an all-or-nothing exercise. You either believe in God or you do not, accept or reject evolution, despise or embrace religion—as if these issues were clearly defined and categorically simple.

However, there is considerable nuance within these arguments. Not only are there different shades of theistic belief, but there are also gradations of atheism. Thus I want to propose a five-point belief/unbelief scale on which we can mark some graduated distinctions. My spectrum of religiosity is not definitive by any means, but it attempts to make an allowance for some of the subtleties in the theism-atheism debate. First I want to define what it means to be *religious*.

## What Makes a Person Religious?

What makes a person religious is belief in and efforts to relate to a Transcendent Spiritual Reality, also understood as the "divine" or "sacred," which incorporates three characteristics:

1. It is a spiritual reality that is not subject to the physical laws and temporal limits of the natural world.

2.  It is an objective reality that transcends the material world, is the source or creator of that material world, and is usually conceived as being *more real* than our material reality.

3.  It is the preeminent *good* to which we must properly orient our moral behavior if we are to attain ultimate fulfillment.

I admit to defining religious sensibility broadly. In my conceptualization, you are considered religious even if your idea of God is indistinct and nebulous, such as in this minimalist definition: "God is a nonphysical being of consciousness and intelligence or wisdom." You fit my definition of religious if you do not specify a particular kind of deity, but believe that you possess a nonmaterial soul or spirit that transcends death. You are religious if you borrow from Eastern traditions in postulating a higher or transcendent self that exists apart from the world of sensory phenomena. Lastly, you are considered religious in any of the above contexts even if you do not express or practice your belief within an organized religious institution.

On the flip side, you are an atheist if you believe that the material world is all that exists; that this world was not created by a spiritual entity of any kind; and that your life force does not survive your death. You are an atheist if you believe that man created religion and that "God" serves humanity (a true believer will always assert that humanity serves God).

## Gradations of Religiosity

In the spectrum of religiosity, there are five options: two theistic, two atheistic, and one agnostic.

- **Militant Atheism:** No God + Evolution = Reductive Purpose
- **Soft Atheism:** No God + Evolution = Human Purpose
- **Agnosticism:** Don't Know, Don't Care

- **Open-Minded Theism:** God + Evolution = Divine Purpose
- **Fundamentalist Theism:** God + Creation = Divine Purpose

## Level 1: Militant Atheism

Atheism has been around since the beginning of Christianity, and doubt has been applied to religious belief at least since the ancient Greeks. The particular strain of unbelief that is called "militant atheism" is found in the recent work of four vociferous religious opponents: the philosopher Daniel Dennett, the academic Sam Harris, the scientist Richard Dawkins, and the journalist Christopher Hitchens.

Militant atheists' bias is revealed by their argument that in religion we find all that is malevolent in humankind. Religion is perceived as being false and dangerous. To militant atheists, the only legitimate response to religious faith is an unremitting assault on its credence using the tools of reason and science. Certainly as a response to Islamic and Christian extremism, atheists have some legitimate points to present. But by including the rest of the religious world in their condemnation and by arguing for the elimination of all religion, they are essentially a mirror image of their fundamentalist enemy.

These uncompromising atheists not only reject God, they reject religion as a cultural institution and seek to eliminate it from society. By turning atheism (a personal belief in the absence of God) into *anti*-theism (a public effort to negate religion), they are taking their creed way beyond its original meaning. In the extreme, they consider religion the "root of all evil" (Dawkins) and that only when religion is eradicated "will we stand a chance of healing the deepest and most dangerous fractures in our world" (Harris).

Militant atheists are scientific materialists who believe that science will someday explain all of reality and that there is no need to resort to supernatural agents. They denounce religion as "superstition" and continue to think that humanity will one day "outgrow" it. According to their scientific creed, human life has no purpose other than evolutionary imperatives. And if one's individual life has any meaning at all, it is based on what the person brings to it. Facing the travails of living and dying without the consolations of religious "delusion" is a hardship, they admit, but is preferable to living an inauthentic life.

## Level 2: Soft Atheism

This is where we find the majority of atheists. These are people who, like me, do not fit the stringent definition of an exclusionary atheist who defers to science and reason to explain all of life. We are atheists not by deliberation but by default—we just have not discovered God and probably never will find God. We are atheists not by conviction, but the lack of conviction: We just do not believe God exists. Soft atheists may have little use for organized religion, but we are still capable of acknowledging the positive contributions of religion to civilization.

While soft atheists reject creationism, at the same time we are unsettled with scientific reductionism and believe in the possibility of a higher human purpose beyond the evolutionary imperatives of survival and reproduction. We do not despise religion; indeed, we may be envious of religion's consolations and aspire to believe in something more meaningful than blind and unguided natural forces. We want to believe that our bodies are more than just DNA-replicating machines. We believe that the whole of life is greater than the sum of its parts, and recognize that science has made minimal progress in assembling those parts to come up with a viable paradigm of the whole.

## Level 3: Agnosticism

This label is often misunderstood as "atheism lite"—a person who is really an atheist but does not want to appear overly assertive about it.

That, however, is not a proper use of the term. You are an agnostic if you believe that God may exist or may not, but that humankind will never know for certain. Another form of agnostic belief consists of people who simply do not care about the existence of God. This is more akin to apathy than atheism and has been labeled "apatheism."

## Level 4: Open-Minded Theism

In this category are people who believe in God *and* evolution; they see no significant disharmony between religion and science. Admittedly, that is because they view evolution as a direct manifestation of the divine and still accept that God created the world. But they do not support a literalist view wherein Earth is merely 6,000 human years old.

There have been many constructive attempts to reconcile belief in God and evolution, including people like Francis Collins (a scientist) and Michael Dowd (a theologian). Collins says that he is "unaware of any irreducible conflict between scientific knowledge about evolution and the idea of a creator God" and further believes that the genetic code is "God's instruction book." Michael Dowd calls himself an "evolutionary evangelist" whose book, *Thank God for Evolution!*, presents the reasons why it is possible to view evolution as a divine process.

Most of the people in this category, of course, are neither scientists nor theologians, but are mainly believers who have learned to live with both religious tradition and scientific fact. You might also be surprised to learn that this category probably represents a majority of Americans. They are content to entertain a compromise such as Dr. Collins's, or a benign, "nonoverlapping magisteria" explanation proposed by Stephen Jay Gould, which respects both disciplines: science as it pertains to the material world and religion as it pertains to the spiritual realm. Being moderates by nature, these people wonder what the whole theist-atheist argument is about. Their priority is not to defeat one or another ideological opponent, but to live a good and purposeful life.

### Level 5: Fundamentalist Theism

The beliefs and practices of the religious fundamentalist are well known. It is important to point out that there is not much difference between the two strains of extremism, one atheistic and the other theistic. In fact, their relationship could almost be expressed as a formal law of group conflict: one group's out-group is the other group's in-group, and vice versa. Each defines itself in terms of the other, specifically as a clear repudiation of the other. In reality, these two groups are symbiotically related and ultimately need each other, gain strength from each other, and paradoxically *become each other*. And one important way in which religious fundamentalists and militant atheists are similar is in misappropriating science.

The militant atheist asserts, incorrectly, that science is capable of determining the nonexistence of God. And the religious fundamentalist, also incorrectly, repudiates the findings of such well-established science as the big bang and evolution in favor of creationism. One asks too much of science and the other not enough.

It is said that when matter and antimatter come into contact, they obliterate each other. That is unfortunately what the two extremist segments of the belief controversy seem to be doing. If it were up to these people, who make up the two ends of a bell-shaped curve, we would never know there is a middle ground.

## Distinguishing Between "Spiritual" and "Religious"

When discussing religion, the question of spirituality invariably arises. Many observers use the terms spirituality and religion interchangeably, but there is a clear distinction.

To be *spiritual* is to *question* our identity, purpose, and destiny—What is the meaning of existence? What happens when we die? Is life worth living? To be spiritual is an existential state of mind that begins within each individual; it is questing for that which connects the self with humanity, nature, and the cosmos. It is the search for what makes life meaningful, valuable, and worth living. It is the desire for unity, transcendence, and the realization of the highest human potential.

To be *religious* is to have found an *answer* to that spiritual quest in a supreme reality that transcends the material world. Thus, I am saying that we are *all* spiritual, but we are not all religious. Everyone, it seems, asks questions of ultimate concern; everyone inquires about what it means to be human. But it is the *answers* to those questions that distinguish the theist from the atheist.

And it is noteworthy that the vast majority of the world's population arrives at a religious and not a secular (naturalistic, materialistic, or scientific) answer to those spiritual questions.

# Militant Atheism's Abuse of Science

If you pay attention to the headlines, you could be excused for believing that science and religion are mutually exclusive and incompatible. In truth, that characterization applies only to a minority of people, the extremists on either side of the debate. But because extremists are usually the most vociferous, theirs tend to be the only voices we hear. Because extremists are the ones writing books and giving speeches, it is easy to think that this conflict reflects the sentiment of the majority of Americans. But it is a manifestation mainly between religious fundamentalists on one end of the spectrum and militant atheists on the other end.

## The Danger of Extremism

Physicist Freeman Dyson said of the extremists: "The media exaggerate their numbers and importance. The media rarely mention the fact that the great majority of religious people belong to moderate denominations that treat science with respect, or the fact that the great majority of scientists treat religion with respect." Thus the battle underway is not between religion and science, but between religious and secular extremists—hardened adherents who believe they hold the exclusive truth.

The enduring lesson of this book is that we should not desire the end of religion or atheism, but the end of ideological dogmatism. Fortunately for the well-being of humanity, the vast majority of people are not comfortable with the fanaticism that infects both sides of the argument. We seek a spiritual and practical center where the best of the religious and secular positions can be preserved. We want to be receptive to the ideals espoused by religion at the same time we embrace the tenets and teachings of science.

Most Americans are not troubled by moderate ideologies. In particular, America is remarkably hospitable to both religion and science, suggesting that there is no substantial contradiction between the two. Conflict is inevitable, however, when either science or religion is used to justify one or another extremist agenda.

Within the past five years, numerous books by militant atheists have highlighted the destructive legacy of fundamentalist religion. In this chapter, I focus on the other end of the ideological spectrum: the extent to which militant atheists misuse science in their effort to challenge the validity of religion as a meaningful paradigm for understanding the world, a perspective I identify as "scientism."

## The Meaning of Scientism

The cultural war playing itself out in the popular press is mainly not between religion and science. (I will show in Chapter 9 that religion and science are largely complementary.) Rather, the ideological struggle is between *religion* and *scientism*. The distinction between science and scientism is subtle, but highly important within this debate. Scientism is the atheistic community's version of fundamentalism; it assumes that only science can describe and understand the world, and that only the material or natural world is real.

Scientism as a belief system has three components:

1. **Naturalism** or **materialism:** The idea that reality can be completely explained as natural phenomena.

2. **Reductionism:** The idea that all natural phenomena can be understood in terms of lower and more elementary levels of existence, all the way down to particle physics (consciousness reduces to biology, biology reduces to chemistry, chemistry reduces to physics, and all physics reduces to the "behavior" of elementary particles and forces).

3. **Atheism:** The ideological implication of materialism and reductionism is a worldview that excludes any conception of the divine—with the corollary that scientific explanation can replace religious understanding of the natural world.

Science and scientism are very different. Science is a method of gathering knowledge of the material world through observation and experimentation. In my view, it is the nature of science to be *agnostic*. Science can say nothing about the existence of God. Scientism, however, is inherently *atheistic*. Scientism espoused by secular extremists misappropriates the verities of science with the explicit aim of repudiating the divine. Thus, it is not science that is incompatible with religion, but scientism that is so strongly opposed to theism. Science is fully capable of evaluating religious experience, but not the spiritual reality behind that experience, which is what scientism purports to do.

As a moderate observer (a centrist atheist and science lover who is sympathetic to religious aspirations), I question the appropriateness of using science to negate religion. In that context, note this statement by militant atheist Steven Weinberg: "Anything scientists can do to weaken the hold of religion may in the end be our greatest contribution to civilization."

I am not questioning the veracity of science, which I embrace wholeheartedly. But I want to challenge militant atheists' subordination of the values-neutral mandate of science to their own objective of rejecting religion. Indeed, once we understand that it is scientism and not science that is opposed to theism, we can envision a genuine rapprochement between the true nature of science and the inestimable value of religion.

Thus scientism is little more than atheism masquerading as science. And the height of scientism is the belief that science actually proves God does not exist. In this regard, note the subtitle to militant atheist Victor Stenger's book *God: The Failed Hypothesis—How Science Shows That God Does Not Exist*. In his book, Stenger argues, "By this moment in time science has advanced sufficiently to be able to make a definitive statement on the existence or nonexistence of God." And his "scientific" conclusion: God is impossible.

## Positioning Science Against Religion

Scientism avers that science is the only reliable and authoritative source of truth, an attitude affirmed by Oxford chemist Peter Atkins, who stated that scientists "are at the summit of knowledge, rationality and intellectual honesty; and there is no reason to suppose that science cannot deal with every aspect of existence." Taken to the logical conclusion, proponents of scientism envision science as the true source of human enlightenment; and the purpose of science is to free humankind from ignorance and false belief, which invariably includes religion.

Many prominent atheists have offered some form of "scientific spirituality" as a replacement for religious sensibility. Here are four examples:

- Carolyn Porco, a researcher, has said, "Let's teach our children about the scientific story of the universe and its incredible richness and beauty. It is already so much more glorious and awesome—and even comforting—than anything offered by any scripture or God concept I know."

- Harvard biologist Edward O. Wilson has written, "Material reality discovered by science already possesses more content and grandeur than all religious cosmologies combined."

- Cornell astronomer Carl Sagan was particularly enthralled with the elegant universe of science: "A religion that stressed the magnificence of the universe as revealed by science might be able to draw forth reserves of reverence and awe hardly tapped by the conventional faiths."

- And physicist Lawrence Krauss declares, "How anyone can suggest that medieval hallucinations [i.e., religious explanations] might spark the imagination more than the actual universe revealed by science" is beyond comprehension.

These are clear instances of strident unbelievers asserting scientism by overtly positioning science against religion. Psychologist Steven Pinker epitomized this ideological opposition when he stated, "Over the millennia, there has been an inexorable trend: the deeper we probe [the existential questions] and the more we learn about the universe, the less reason there is to believe in God." And James Watson, co-discoverer of DNA, has declared that "one of the greatest gifts science has brought to the world is the continuing elimination of the supernatural." In other words, it is a zero-sum universe where more science equals less religion.

All the most fervent proponents of atheism (including Dawkins and Dennett, Harris and Hitchens) propose that naturalistic explanations for existence are superior to religious-mythical explanations. However, by establishing an oppositional relationship between religious meaning and scientific understanding, militant atheists do not engender a conciliatory climate. Rather, to the extent that atheists antagonistically position science against religion, they actually produce the opposite effect to the one intended: Religious people's confidence in science is undermined; science becomes the "enemy." The fundamental irony that results from pitting science against religion is that it serves to harden the extremists on the other side of the debate—an outcome we see playing out in American classrooms and courtrooms, in the mass media and the public square.

Many atheists claim that the universe as understood by science is full of exalted wonder, which can be experienced just by looking up at the heavens with a small telescope. But they do not understand that for the religious person there is an enormous difference between the lifeless beauty of the natural cosmos revealed by science and the fully alive conception of the cosmos revered by believers. Militant atheists do not understand that religious answers to spiritual questions may not conform to the facts of science, but for believers they offer a sense of meaning and transcendence that scientific explanations cannot. The straightforward, mechanistic explanation for natural phenomena does not lead believers to an emotional epiphany or spiritual peak experience. Believers do not deny the grandeur of the star-studded night sky, but for them it cannot compare to the experience of looking upward to the religiously inspired ceiling of the Sistine Chapel.

Richard Dawkins has also made the case that cosmic meaning can be derived from scientific conceptions of the world. He writes of "the feeling of awed wonder that science can give us" as "one of the highest experiences of which the human psyche is capable." I do not doubt that Dawkins has had many spiritually moving experiences through science, but it may be presumptuous to expect that religious believers can be so enthralled. Dawkins claims, "If Bach had been brought up in an atheistic culture, he might have produced oratorios just as sublime, but inspired by the universe, by the galaxy, by plate tectonics." But something tells me that plate tectonics would not have inspired Bach to compose "St. Matthew Passion."

## Man's Place in the Universe

People are naturally driven by *biophilia,* defined by Erich Fromm as a passionate love of life and a primordial urge to see the world as profoundly alive. Taking biophilia to its highest expression, most people are inclined to see behind the wondrous complexity and grandeur of nature a beneficent, intelligent, and transcendent God.

But that is not the world science reveals. Science teaches that the universe is a cold and empty place dominated by impersonal and mechanistic forces; that culture, religion, and morality are reduced to the twin evolutionary imperatives of preservation and procreation; and that the most successful form of life on Earth are not the humans who have existed for only a geological instant, but bacteria that have dominated the planet for almost four billion years. According to science, the flip side of the immensity of the universe is the *smallness* of human life.

Here is what several prominent scientists have said about man's place in the universe as revealed by science:

- Nobel biologist Jacques Monod: "If man accepts the message of science in its full significance, he must at last discover his total solitude, his fundamental isolation."
- Eminent cosmologist Stephen Hawking: "The human race is just chemical scum on a moderate-sized planet."

- Nobel laureate Francis Crick: "Your joys and your sorrows, your memories and ambitions, your sense of personal identity and free will are in fact no more than the behavior of a vast assembly of nerve cells and their associated molecules."

- Biologist E. O. Wilson: "The individual organism is only the vehicle of genes, part of an elaborate device to preserve and spread them with the least possible perturbation. The organism is only DNA's way of making more DNA."

Such reductionism undermines the foundational religious beliefs on which much of humankind relies for its sense of significance and transcendence. Realizing that humans are just vehicles for DNA replication and that our most cherished experiences are explained by scientific materialism hardly inspires believers to hold a positive outlook on life.

The French mathematician Blaise Pascal (1623–1662), a deeply religious man, was filled with dread when he contemplated the "eternal silence" of the material universe as revealed by science:

> When I see the blind and wretched state of men, when I survey the whole universe in its deadness, and man left to himself with no light, as though lost in this corner of the universe without knowing who put him there, what he has to do, or what will become of him when he dies, incapable of knowing anything, I am moved to terror, like a man transported in his sleep to some terrifying desert island, who wakes up quite lost, with no means to escape.

It is true that science makes humans almost omnipotent in a material sense. But it leaves humans knowing they are still finite and fragile beings, the very condition people seek to rise above through religion.

In the demythologized world of science, the sense of cosmic purpose and specialness conferred by religion is nowhere to be found. Man is confronted by his own insignificance and eventual extinction.

For the deeply religious, scientific explanations do not inspire a sense of meaning or purpose because they suggest, essentially, that *there is no meaning or purpose* in the universe. Richard Dawkins has said repeatedly that the materialist universe we observe "has precisely the properties we should expect if there is, at bottom, no design, no purpose, no evil and no good, nothing but blind, pitiless indifference."

For religionists, therefore, the scientific worldview desacralizes nature, leaving it like a machine to be observed and manipulated, rather than an object of reverence as a creation of God. For this reason, the scientific response disappoints religious believers. Looking up to the night sky and feeling the immensity of existence is only the beginning of the religious quest for transcendence. For believers, *wonder* has to be met with *oneness*, a sense that the universe embraces them. But science does not provide a satisfactory way for believers to feel at home in the universe. That is why so many people turn to religion.

## Explaining Religion Away

It has been said that the history of science—from Copernicus to Darwin to Freud to Skinner—can be viewed as an ongoing process of shattering the pedestals upon which humankind has maintained its existential vanity, the idea that we humans are a special creation—even a divine creation. And perhaps the greatest pedestal to tear down is God. There is no question that a diverse group of scientists has been gunning for religion. By explaining religion in terms of science, they feel they can explain religion *away*. Scientific attempts to illuminate religious experience take two forms: explanations from evolutionary psychology and neurochemistry.

When science examines religious experience, it focuses only on biology, brain chemistry, and genetics. If taken too far, this kind of analysis can undermine the validity of believer experience. The more that religion can be found *inside* the human body and brain, the less it seems that religion has an objective source *outside*. Research like this not only questions the reality of God and the spiritual realm, but also attempts to reduce religion to imaginary experiences, evolutionary mistakes, genetic adaptive "misfirings," psychedelic phenomena, and psychosis.

## Understanding Religion: Evolution

A number of scientists have offered theories of how natural selection produced religion. According to evolutionary experts, there is no question about human behavior that cannot be explained by looking at the survival strategies of hunter-gatherer societies as well as examining the behavior of social animals.

In his book *On Human Nature*, Edward O. Wilson has said that "the highest forms of religious practice" are essentially a genetic adaptation and that "religion is subject to the explanations of the natural sciences" as a "wholly material phenomenon." In *Consilience*, Wilson reiterated that "Much if not all religious behavior could have arisen from evolution by natural selection." Wilson's efforts to explain religion in terms of evolution is rooted in his desire to undermine religion's power: "If religion can be systematically analyzed as a product of the brain's evolution, its power as an external source of morality will be gone forever." To prove his point, Wilson proceeds to cite examples from packs of wolves and troops of rhesus monkeys to show that religion has its roots in the adaptive behavior of social animals.

In a different conceptualization, anthropologist Stewart Guthrie takes something as complex as religion and reduces it to anthropomorphism: projecting humanlike qualities onto the natural world.

According to Guthrie, God is an illusion and anthropomorphism is an adaptive trait that enhanced our ancestors' chances for survival. Over millennia, as natural selection bolstered our unconscious anthropomorphic tendencies, they reached beyond specific objects and events to encompass all of nature until we persuaded ourselves that "the entire world of our experience is merely a show staged by some master dramatist," which is to say, God.

We also have the recent theory posited by Scott Atran and other evolutionary scientists that religion is a "spandrel"—that is, "a non-adaptive side consequence" (read: accident) of other more essential and expedient evolutionary traits. Richard Dawkins shares the view: "I am one of an increasing number of biologists who see religion as a *by-product* of something else." Thus, we are to believe that all the majesty and mystery of religion; all its temples, wisdom, art, worship, ceremonies, and myths; all its complexity and diversity—are just a fortuitous and extraneous side-product of something else more important to evolution (*what*, exactly, is not specified).

These various ideas depend heavily on "evolutionary psychology," the field that says every behavior, directly or indirectly, exists to enhance the odds that one's genes will be passed on. Evolutionary psychology is an intellectual instance where if you have a hammer, everything looks like a nail. As biologist Jerry Coyne has said "Evolutionary psychology suffers from the scientific equivalent of megalomania. Most of its adherents are convinced that virtually every human action or feeling was put directly into our brains by natural selection." Evolutionary psychology certainly makes sense when used to explain human mate choice, for example, but seems implausible when used to explain complex cultural phenomena such as religion. Devout believers would say they are religious because they seek to connect with and serve God, not to reproduce their genes.

## Understanding Religion: Brain Chemistry

If natural selection is responsible for the development of religious behavior, brain scientists are interested in understanding the neural substratum that explains how this evolutionary adaptation is mediated by the brain. In this materialist view, believers perceive "God" because their brains have evolved to produce religious faith. There is little agreement about how this happens; this is but another instance where complex and multifaceted behavior is reduced to simplistic physiological phenomena. Put a magnetic helmet around people's heads, they begin to think they're having a spiritual epiphany. If people suffer from temporal lobe epilepsy, they may show signs of hyper-religiosity. If one part of their brain is overexcited, people begin to believe they are conversing with God.

Neuroscientist Patrick McNamara works with people who suffer from Parkinson's Disease, which is characterized by low levels of the neurotransmitter dopamine in certain parts of the brain. He made the observation that those with Parkinson's exhibit lower levels of religiosity than healthy individuals, and that the difference seemed to correlate with the disease's severity. He therefore suspects a link between religion and dopamine levels.

Neuroscientist Michael Persinger claims he induced religious experiences in subjects by stimulating specific regions of their brains with electromagnetic pulses. Our sense of self is ordinarily mediated by the brain's left hemisphere, specifically by the left temporal lobe. When the brain is mildly disrupted—by head injury or psychological trauma—our left-brain self may interpret activity within the right hemisphere as another self, or what Persinger calls a "sensed presence," such as a supernatural being. Religion or the experience of God, Persinger suggests, is thus a cerebral mistake.

Andrew Newberg, a neuroscientist, scanned the brains of more than 20 adherents of spiritual practices, including Christian prayer and Tibetan Buddhist meditation, to understand the brain chemistry of mystical experiences. Newberg's scans showed that the subjects' neural activity decreases in the region at the top and rear of the brain called the posterior superior parietal lobe. Newberg hypothesizes that suppressed activity in this brain region could trigger a mystical experience by heightening a sense of unity with the external world, thus diminishing a person's sense of subject-object duality.

Neuroscientist Michael Gazzaniga has the idea that religious experience is a manifestation of a disease state—specifically, temporal lobe epilepsy (TLE). TLE patients often display a set of characteristics even when they are not seizing, characteristics that may result from damage to the temporal lobe of the brain. "Most interesting about TLE is the prevalence of religious experiences during seizures and religiosity in the periods between seizures. If seizures can cause religious experience, and seizures are merely an overexcitement of brain tissue, then it is possible, and indeed likely, that religiosity could have an organic basis within the normally functioning brain."

## Religionists' Response

Very few religious people actually oppose the progression of science. What they object to is militant atheists' presentation of science as inherently antireligious. To the extent that militant atheists use science to deny the divine, religious fundamentalists see in science the contradiction of their most cherished beliefs. When prominent atheist-scientists claim religion is a "delusion" that "poisons everything" and is the "root of all evil," it is easy to understand why religious people feel that science threatens their beliefs.

But positioning science against religion, as militant atheists do, does not diminish the power of religion one bit. In fact, it often accomplishes the opposite: intensifying religionists' antipathy to science. In response we have religious extremists striving to "disprove" evolution through their own distortions of science (presenting so-called "creation science"; exaggerating the "gaps" that exist in the fossil record; misusing the term "theory," which in science nomenclature does not mean something tentative or provisional). By denying the reality of evolution (such as disputing that life on Earth is 3.5 billion years old), biblical literalists are helping to perpetuate the science-and-religion opposition just as much as secular extremists who manipulate science to deny the existence of God.

It is clear that for religious adherents, a scripture based on the findings of science cannot delineate an overarching destiny for humankind from which flow civilization's highest ideals or most enduring values. When scientific theory does acknowledge an overriding purpose to human existence, it is not one of great moral accomplishments or venerable cultural monuments. Evolutionary theory allows only for an endless circle of survival and reproduction in the service of more survival and reproduction. And in that, humans are not the masterpiece of divine creation; instead, humanity is an unintended offshoot of a process that makes no distinction between *Homo sapiens* and more elementary living beings.

By comparison, for most people the religious narrative confers greater meaning. Religion works for the majority because it makes the universe comprehensible to a mind that seeks *transcendent value* above all else. Indeed, reservations about scientism are not limited to religious fundamentalists. The great physicist Erwin Schrodinger understood that science falls short as a method to create meaning: "The scientific picture of the world around me is very deficient" he said. "It gives me a lot of factual information, puts all our experience in a magnificently consistent order, but is ghastly silent about all that is really near to our heart, that really matters to us. It knows nothing of beauty and ugly, good or bad, God or eternity." Schrodinger's contemporary, physicist Wolfgang Pauli, concurred when he lamented "the lack of soul" that characterizes the modern scientific conception of the world.

I believe that everyone is spiritual because we all ask the same timeless questions about existence. And we all have a spiritual experience when we contemplate the grandeur of the visible universe. The issue is whether one turns to a religious or materialist explanation to that spiritual quest; whether one sees a Transcendent Spiritual Reality behind the awesome natural beauty of the universe, or only the big bang and evolution.

People do not want merely to look up at the star-studded night sky and feel "in the presence" of infinity; they need to feel *connected* to the cosmos in a way that affirms the sanctity of their existence. Humans need to understand that their personal destiny is bound up with the drama of the universe. Hence, in the religious person's worldview: Science places humanity on the periphery of the universe, while religion puts humans in the *center*. In science life is an accident; in religion life is a *miracle*. Science emphasizes humanity's finitude; religion prepares humans for *eternity*. For those reasons, the majority of people turn to religion rather than science to understand their place in the universe.

In the next chapter, I will show that for the majority of Americans, religion and science are not at war with each other, and that for moderate believers and moderate atheists, religion and science can be integral parts of one fulfilling life.

# Reconciling Religion and Science

Ever since the eighteenth-century Enlightenment, which proclaimed the inexorable secularization of society, it has generally been assumed that the advance of scientific understanding, with its rational rigors grounded in empirical knowledge, would supersede religious authority based on unchallenged faith. Religion, presumably, belonged to the primitive past, while secular science and technology belonged to the mature future. Yet today we see the flourishing of both.

In his book *A Secular Age*, Charles Taylor observed that the West has evolved from a "society in which it was virtually impossible not to believe in God, to one in which faith, even for the staunchest believer, is one human possibility among others." But we have also learned that the secular age, characterized by the rise of several nonreligious ideas and their corresponding institutions—individuality (capitalism), human rights (democracy), and naturalism (science)—is not an alternative to God and does not preclude God. Religion may have lost mind-share to secular institutions, but it did not disappear.

In the past, informed observers have emphasized the conflict between science and religion at the expense of what they have in common.

In this chapter, I will describe four ways of thinking about the science-religion relationship. And I will ultimately show that on the deepest level modern science and religion are not opposites—they arise from the same urge toward progress, transcendence, and salvation found within the human spirit.

## The Emergence of Science from Religion

It is assumed that science and religion have always been in conflict. However, there was a time not long ago when all human activity was permeated with the divine and all cultural expressions were *devotional*: art, music, and philosophy, to be sure, but also reason, science, and technology. The great irony of the science-religion debate is that science emerged from religion, specifically in the West. According to Rodney Stark, a prominent historian of religion, "Not only were science and religion compatible, they were inseparable—the rise of science was achieved by deeply religious Christian scholars." For early scientists, almost all of whom were very religious, scientific investigation was regarded as an appropriate way to be closer to God's creation.

While today Christians see God as upholding the natural order from beyond the universe and physicists think of their laws as inhabiting a realm of mathematical relationships, in Newton's time they were thought to be one and the same: The mathematical relationships of physics were seen as expressions of God's handiwork. Originally called the mechanical arts, science and technology were endowed with spiritual significance and divine purpose.

Christianity embraced the idea of an ordered cosmos that embodied the rationality of God the creator. That man was made in the image or likeness of God meant that man held a spark of divine reason, giving him the power to understand the laws of nature. Francis Bacon, a devoutly religious man, argued that through the God-given power of discovery man could fulfill the divine mandate to establish dominion over creation and even restore a new kind of Eden.

Through the fourteenth century, science and religion were essentially united. Natural philosophers (they were not called scientists until the nineteenth century) were often theologically inspired, and up until the twentieth century, scientists were steeped in religious teachings. Robert Boyle (1627–1691) said that science is a religious task, revealing "the admirable workmanship which God displayed in the universe." Isaac Newton (1642–1726) first got the idea of absolute, universal, immutable laws from the Christian doctrine that God created the world and ordered it in a rational way: "This most beautiful system of the sun, planets, and comets could only proceed from the counsel and dominion of an Intelligent Powerful Being." And Johannes Kepler (1571–1630) saw the universe in the same way: "I wanted to become a theologian. Now, however, I behold how through my effort God is being celebrated through astronomy."

It makes sense that when Christian scholars saw scientific discoveries as another form of divine revelation, they were proponents of science. So long as scientific inquiry focused on the inner workings of the natural world, it did not contradict the religious understanding that everything is a result of God's creativity. And that is precisely the irony: Science emerged as a child of religion only to chart an independent path from its parent and challenge religion on many existential questions. Once science began to veer in a direction that would contradict church teachings and challenge the biblical interpretations of human origins, conflict was inevitable. Darwinian theory in particular threatened the core of Christian thought, namely, the purposefulness of the world, human specialness, the distinctive human moral capacity, and the drama of Creation and the Fall.

By the eighteenth century, the study of nature, including human nature, was brought under the scientific model. In time there were two truths, one of the natural world and the other of the spiritual world; one rational and the other dependent on faith in divine revelation. The Enlightenment and the Scientific Revolution made it possible to think about the material world without reference to any transcendent power. The possibility of understanding the world without reference to God is one of the defining features of the modern era.

As a consequence, each modern generation has had its secular prophet predicting, even promising, the end of religion. As recently as 1968, for example, the religious sociologist Peter Berger triumphantly asserted that, by "the twenty-first century, religious believers are likely to be found only in small sects, huddled together to resist a worldwide secular culture." This idea was based on the mistaken assumption that the secular-religion relationship is a zero-sum dynamic: that more of one (secular explanation) necessarily means less of the other (religious understanding).

This clearly has not been the case, to the point where four science-religion relationship models prevail in our world today:

- **Irreconcilable Conflict:** This is the most visible model by virtue of the extremist positions held by acolytes on either side of the debate.
- **Mutual Respect:** This widely accepted model attempts to mitigate conflict by emphasizing that science and religion represent distinctive domains of experience and knowledge.
- **Integration:** In this model, moderate religionists make a sincere and constructive effort to accommodate science and evolution.
- **Shared Humanism:** This model shows that religion and science share the same ultimate concern: the flourishing of humanity.

# Irreconcilable Conflict

The science-and-religion relationship model that dominates the cultural agenda is characterized by an irreconcilable conflict between extremists on both sides of the ideological spectrum: biblical literalists and creationists versus militant atheists and scientific materialists.

Eminent theologian Paul Tillich recognized that the conflict between science and religion is sustained and accentuated by two extremist positions: "It is obvious that a theology which interprets the biblical story of creation as a scientific description of an event that happened once upon a time interferes with methodologically controlled scientific work; and that a theory of evolution that interprets man's descent from older forms of life in a way that removes the infinite [contradicts the core belief of religion]." Physicist Freeman Dyson also noted the ideological nature of this conflict: "Trouble arises when either science or religion claims universal jurisdiction, when either religious or scientific dogma claims to be infallible. Religious creationists and scientific materialists are equally dogmatic and insensitive. By their arrogance they bring both science and religion into disrepute."

It is unfortunate that the vehemence of both sides only serves to perpetuate the conflict. The strident efforts of militant atheists are certain to antagonize religionists, which lead to counterdefensive efforts by religionists that are invariably seen as offensive by atheists, and so on. Each group sees the other as an existential threat.

On the one side we have a doctrine that uses the tools of science to deny the existence of God—what I have previously called scientism. As such, it is a rival belief system to theism and reaches beyond testable science. Science by itself is a method, not a creed. Science is a way of formulating knowledge of the natural world; it is not a belief system and thus not a refutation of anything outside the natural world. On the enduring mysteries of divinity, science remains officially agnostic. Yet it is because scientism seeks to deny the divine that the religious fundamentalist sees in science the negation of his most revered beliefs. Thus statements like this one by Richard Dawkins can only further polarize the debate: "Religions have historically always attempted to answer questions that properly belong to science." Not only is this a narrow view of religion, but also of science.

On the other side are creationists and biblical literalists who use any ploy to introduce divine origins into the science curriculum of public schools. In a sense biblical literalists are saying that, because we as a society consider science the final word on reality, by placing the teachings of religion outside the realm of science we are belittling the veracity of religion. It would be fine if creationists left the idea of teaching "intelligent design" to the nonscience curriculum—theology, philosophy, and history. But in attempting to place creationism into the science classroom, they are accentuating the conflict between religion and science.

I am of the mind that only science should be taught in science classes, and that creationism is definitely not science. This is yet another unfortunate instance of religion encroaching upon science, which is no more justified than science encroaching upon religion. To the extent that biblical literalists seek to teach some form of creationism in science class, they are in a sense declaring war on science.

Is it any surprise that reasonable people are made to feel they must choose between two incompatible extremes: to deny the trustworthiness of science or repudiate the value of religion? Many Americans are against science because they perceive that science is against religion, which is decidedly not true. Rather it is scientism—atheism in the guise of science—that is antireligious.

In the science-religion conflict model, the only way there can be a resolution among extremists is in defeat of the other side: Either religion becomes a wholly owned subsidiary of Evolution Inc., or scientists buy into what I call the Flintstones Fallacy that has humans and dinosaurs coexisting.

In the minds of extremists, however, there is little hope for a rapprochement. The tragedy, again, is that a polarized, competitive view debases both science *and* religion. Scientific materialists disrespect religion, to be sure, but they also abuse science. And biblical literalists disparage science, to be sure, but they also diminish religion. Ultimately, when devout believers deny the big bang and evolution, this is not religion; it is ignorance. And when militant atheists claim that natural empiricism invalidates spiritual beliefs, this is not science; it is arrogance.

The additional unfortunate aspect of this conflict is that it is not restricted to the intellectual, academic, or pedagogical realms. In the United States, so-called culture wars are not only fought in newspaper columns and town hall meetings, they are also fought in the courts. And excluding the issue of abortion, no cultural issue occupies the courts more than what gets taught in science classrooms—going way back to the Scopes trial in 1925. Additionally, the legal argumentation surrounding the evolution-creationism issue only serves to amplify the conflict in the popular mind—to the point where science scholars are seen arguing their respective positions in the mass media and prominent political figures are called upon to make public pronouncements one way or another.

And the media attention is not flattering to either side of the debate. "The Evolution Wars" was how *Time* magazine titled its article devoted to a recent court case. "Fight the Good Fight" was how *New Scientist* headlined its treatment. And *Rolling Stone's* coverage was addressed as "Darwinian Warfare." Rather than helping people to reach a compromise, relegating this issue to the courts and the media magnifies the contentiousness to the point where an accommodation becomes all the more difficult to achieve.

## Mutual Respect

As we have seen, the "conflict" as defined by the extremists on either side of the debate leaves no room for compromise. It is, quite simply, a no-win situation.

In the spirit of reconciliation, the famous evolutionary biologist Stephen Jay Gould developed the idea of "respectful noninterference," whereby science and religion occupy distinct "nonoverlapping magisteria" or domains. In Gould's model, "Science tries to document the factual character of the natural world, and to develop theories that coordinate and explain these facts. Religion operates in the equally important, but utterly different, realm of human purposes, meanings and values."

Gould was essentially saying that if the two disciplines never interact, there can never be any conflict. I refer to Gould's two domains as lowercase "truth" and uppercase "Truth"—the former applies to science, which tries to document the factual character of the natural world and develop theories that explain those facts; the latter pertains to religion (as well as philosophy), the realm of human purposes and values. Gould was adamant that science and religion were not to encroach upon the other's realm and that they could not be integrated: "I do not see how science and religion could be unified, or even synthesized, under any common scheme of explanation or analysis; but I also do not understand why the two enterprises should experience any conflict."

The problem with the "nonoverlapping" paradigm is that religion and science are still seen as incompatible. This represents an agreement to disagree, to be civil, but ultimately not to take each other very seriously. And it suggests that there is no way for the two to relate to each other in any meaningful manner. The fact that so many people accept Gould's idea suggests how much people perceive the two realms to be incompatible and even antagonistic, and how much people desire a cessation of hostilities.

While noninterference is preferable to the inherent conflict model, my concern is that it is just a holding pattern. Gould's notion of nonoverlapping domains suggests that the two are neighbors that have nothing to do with each other. He never spelled out how they may interrelate, or whether they should. Insofar as most Americans are both religious and secular, however, I would argue that we can do a little more than just compartmentalize the two. When we say science and religion are separate, we mean that in terms of mutual respect. They are different, and those differences should be respected on both sides.

The mutual respect model is the most widely practiced and is shared by physicist Freeman Dyson:

> *Science and religion are two windows that people look through,*
> *trying to understand the big universe outside, trying to under-*
> *stand why we are here. The two windows give different views,*
> *but they look out at the same universe. Both views are one-*
> *sided, neither is complete. Both leave out essential features of*
> *the real world. And both are worthy of respect.*

Pope John Paul II embraced this model when, in 1996, he issued a statement proclaiming that evolution is "more than just a hypothesis" and is compatible with Christian faith. Thus the Vatican is permitting Catholics to accept the evolution of the human body—so long as it does not contradict the divine creation of the human soul.

The National Academy of Sciences also endorses a view that science and religion need not be in conflict. In one report, "Teaching about Evolution and the Nature of Science," the organization proclaimed:

> *At the root of the apparent conflict between some religions*
> *and evolution is a misunderstanding of the critical difference*
> *between religious and scientific ways of knowing. Religions*
> *and science answer different questions about the world.*
> *Whether there is a purpose to the universe or a purpose for*
> *human existence are not questions for science. Religious and*
> *scientific ways of knowing have played, and will continue to*
> *play, significant roles in human history.*

So if the Pope and the National Academy can agree, where's the reason for conflict? In affirming science and religion as two different realms of knowledge, the nonoverlapping model makes some very important pronouncements: Science cannot say with certainty there is no spiritual world. What science discovers is not necessarily the whole of reality, and that should not cast doubt on what science does not discover. The success of science in its own domain does not negate other domains where its instruments are silent. Science cannot assign meaning or purpose to the world it explores. Questions about good and evil, about the meaning and purpose of existence, have no place in science because they cannot be addressed by the scientific method.

## Integration

In the integration model, we acknowledge that science and religion are two dimensions of people's lives, and thus cannot be compartmentalized. Robert Bellah speaks to this inextricable relationship:

> *Science and religion have different purposes, different limitations, different modes of actions. But they are both part of every culture and every person. They need to exist in some vital and healthy whole in which each is integral. This means not simply a tacit agreement to ignore each other but open interchange between them with all the possibilities of mutual growth and transformation that entails.*

It is plausible to think that science and religion can engage in a dialogue and can in fact enhance each other to some extent, but the nature of that relationship depends on the person holding the beliefs. We must look at each of two groups separately: religious believers and nonbelievers.

## How Believers Integrate Science and Religion

Religious scientists, who represent a minority among all scientists, are inclined to see the "language of God" in the advancement of science. That was the term used by Francis Collins, former head of the Human Genome Project, who helped write a speech that President Clinton gave at the announcement of the first sequencing of the human genome: "Today, we are learning the language in which God created life. We are gaining ever more awe for the complexity, the beauty, and the wonder of God's most divine and sacred gift."

It is possible for religious moderates to reconcile God and science, much the way Newton and other religious scientists did in previous centuries. These are people who say that scientific knowledge can strengthen faith in God, not eradicate it, because, like their scientific predecessors, it reveals the works of God through his creation. The Bible for these people, however, is not true to the literal word; rather, it is metaphor and symbolism. For these scientists and the millions of laypeople who are in accord, the only aspect of faith that Darwin challenges is literalism, not true religiosity.

For Collins, there is no contradiction between the conclusions derived from rigorous scientific explanation and the acceptance of God. Collins considers this a profound effort at reconciliation, but as I will explain it is not a true compromise because it is predicated on subordinating the big bang and evolution to one true God. Collins writes in his book, *The Language of God*, "At the moment of the creation of the universe, God could also have activated evolution, with full knowledge of how it would turn out." He says further, "The God of the Bible is also the God of the genome. He can be worshipped in the cathedral or in the laboratory."

This is a great step to accommodation because it implies that the Bible is not a literal text, but to some extent an allegorical and metaphorical text. Another God-evolution conciliator is Rev. Michael Dowd, who has been called an "evolutionary evangelist." In his book *Thank God for Evolution!*, Dowd presents his idea of "sacred evolution." The more he learned about evolution, the more he saw it as pointing toward God. Dowd says that by embracing evolution, "I wasn't giving up something, I was gaining something." Like Newton and Kepler, Dowd believes "science is showing us what God is revealing."

The problem, of course, is that this kind of "reconciliation" is not appropriate for all moderates in the debate. Collins is enthusiastic about his reconciliation of religion and science, but it is hugely unsatisfying to the nonbeliever. He is saying: All we have to do is believe in God as the creator of the universe and evolution, and the issue is solved. While this is an admirable way for believers to reconcile religion and science, it is unfortunately not a solution that nonbelievers can accept. For a secularist, the human genome is not the language of God; it is the language of biology. As moderate as Collins's and Dowd's positions appear, they still attribute everything to God, which an atheist cannot accept. So this raises the question: Can an atheist incorporate religion into his life?

## The Predicament of Nonbelievers

I wish I had a magical answer to that question, but I do not. A materialist, even a moderate one, does not accept any notion of the divine. It's not that we do not want to believe in the divine, it's that we cannot. So whatever religion offers to a moderate unbeliever has to be defined in the context of the secular world. While it seems a small concession, moderate secularists can acknowledge the religious foundations for many of our most cherished institutions and moral precepts. We can further believe that religion continues to enhance and enrich our secular culture, and that religious people continue to be a force for good through various faith-based works.

I agree with Collins when he says, "Science is the only reliable way to understand the natural world. But science is powerless to answer questions such as 'Why did the universe come into being?' 'What is the meaning of human existence?' 'What happens after we die?'" The problem is that God-centric answers to these questions, as Collins offers, are not something a moderate atheist can embrace.

Many believers tell me that I should just "open" myself to the rationality of God and relinquish the irrationality of atheism; but for me that remains near impossible at this point. I come back to what I said earlier: This is not a choice. No decision based on faith is a choice. We may rationalize after the fact, but I do not see deliberation working. Indeed, if it was only a matter of the "evidence," then people should be converted from one side of the debate to the other all the time, which is clearly not the case. That is why the "10 proofs that God exists" are no more persuasive to an atheist than the "10 proofs that God does not exist" are to the believer.

I acknowledge the limitations of the scientific materialist worldview. But I cannot go outside of it, as much as I want to. And I will not engage in the reverse psychology of making my atheism into a virtue. Thus I am still left with the incessant issue of the inadequacy of science to answer the questions about life, death, and destiny. So I am betwixt and between: I recognize that science cannot answer those questions to the satisfaction of my spiritual needs, but I am unable to believe in the answer provided by religion. This is an interesting existential situation in which to find myself, and I do not think that I am the only one.

Yet I believe that science and religion can indeed be affirmed within the secularist's mind. And in so doing, extremist theism and militant atheism will both be cast aside in favor of something more humanistic.

## Shared Vision of Humanism

To the chagrin of militant atheists, religion is not a vestige of an earlier phase of human development that would wither away as society became more secular and scientific. Religion is just as much a component of modern human life as is science. And there is no doubt that both science and religion are immensely beneficial for humanity.

Although they come at it from different ontological perspectives, science and religion are both predicated on the perfectibility of humankind. Certain observers, like Chris Hedges and Ernest Becker, have a difficult time with this idea; they assert that it is pure hubris and the real source of human evil. In his book *I Don't Believe in Atheists*, Hedges writes, "The utopian dream of a perfect society and a perfect human being, the idea that we are moving toward collective salvation, is one of the most dangerous legacies of the Christian faith and the Enlightenment." And in his book *Escape from Evil*, Becker tried to show that it was man's efforts to transcend his limitations, especially mortality, that has been the source of humanity's destructiveness. But I believe that seeking to perfect ourselves is an essential part of human nature. In some instances, it may have brought us the worst of consequences, but mainly it has brought us the best, and we will continue to improve upon earlier endeavors.

I think we can begin to envision a true rapprochement between moderate secularists and religionists. Both science and religion have something meaningful to contribute to a Universal Ethic. What is characteristic of Western religion today is that while it remains by definition God-centric, it is increasingly human centered. Much of contemporary religion is less about God and more about humanity. And while religion still sees man as a creature in relation to the creator God, today the nature of that relationship is more a partnership than one of unquestioned obedience. Increasingly, modern religion is humanistic, and the same can be said of science.

I have previously emphasized that science does not speak to ethics and values. But that is not entirely correct as a distinction must be made between the purity of the scientific method and the impetus behind the scientific enterprise. The scientific method is truly values-neutral; it is dedicated only to understanding the natural world. The institution we call science, on the other hand, is indeed motivated by a genuine desire to improve the human condition: increasing food yields, curing disease, overcoming the conditions that foster poverty, understanding the reasons for criminal behavior, distributing low-cost personal computers to poor children—the list of science's humanistic aims is endless. In fact, for every major problem that humans face, invariably there is a science and/or technology component to the solution.

Thus, the two disciplines—science and religion—continue to express humanity's teleological quest for progress and perfection: "the best and most complete form of goodness," in Aristotle's words. Science and religion come from the same human aspiration—the quest for transcendence and salvation. Both disciplines strive to understand the essence of the universe, the "language of God." And in a sense, both seek to recover humankind's "lost divinity." Through technological advancement, humans seek understanding of the universe and deliverance from our earthly existence. Science may tell us that nothing exists beyond the natural realm, but at the same time it seeks to push man *above* nature to omniscience (information technology), immortality (medical science), and omnipotence (mechanical, electrical, quantum engineering). Thus technology and the power of reason have come to be identified with progress and the perfectibility of man—a "secular eschatology" where man is liberated from his earthly limitations.

I would like to see science and religion *share* a vision for humanity because I believe they are motivated by the same overarching purpose. I want to foster an interdisciplinary dialogue between science and the various religions. We know that religion and science at their best possess the common vision to uplift and enhance humankind. They are each capable of contributing something distinctive, and their common mission means they are allies, not enemies.

## The State of Science in America

Like many people, I lament our nation's lagging academic performance in the scientific disciplines. Antiscience is no more useful than anti-religion. But making science into a competing ideology to religion is not the way to address this problem. Telling people that their deepest beliefs are wrong and, worse, silly, does not endear scientists to the majority. Most scientists are respectful of religious sentiments, but some, such as Dawkins, Harris, and Weinberg, exhibit outright contempt.

In survey after survey, U.S. students perform below the international average in math and science. In a 2001 National Science Foundation survey of scientific literacy, 53 percent of American adults were unaware that the last dinosaur died before the first human came into being. Just 50 percent knew that Earth orbits the sun and takes a year to do so. And to the consternation of scientists, surveys also indicate that only a minority of Americans accept evolution as biologists understand it.

Atheists must recognize that in the competition between science and religion—a contest that militant atheists accentuate—in the public mind, religion will almost always win. The implications are far-reaching, especially for engineering, technology, and business competitiveness. It is unfortunate that when militant atheists pit science against religion and champion scientism (essentially atheism masquerading as science), this only invites a reactionary response from religionists.

We live in a time when too few people are science literate. But rather than worrying about whether intelligent design finds its way into science curricula, secularists should be more concerned about the way science is taught in schools. The fact that *CSI* is the inspiration for many high school science majors is pathetic. And contrary to what atheists think, this predicament has less to do with religion and more to do with the uninspiring methods used to get students interested in science. I hated science in high school and college. Once I began to read science presented by good writers, I discovered a love for science (even if I remain intimidated by the technical and mathematical aspects of it).

By manipulating science in an effort to undermine religion, atheists are making people more hostile to science when our nation needs all the home-grown scientists we can train. Making science into a competing ideology to religion is not the way to augment science graduate students. Indeed, the conflict between science and religion that is being staged in public is a huge distraction. The sooner we understand that religion and science are essential for a civilized society, the more civilized our society will be.

Cynics can argue that science has helped create many universal problems (global warming, overpopulation, pollution), but all those problems were the result of science's *success*, and few of us are prepared to turn back the clock on prosperity if that were the only way to solve those problems. The only real solution to the problems borne by science is still *more science*—plus some help from religious ethicists.

What will make more people accept science? It does not require reconciliation with creationism—not at all. But we do face the need to further humanize science. It is true that the methods of science do not need a conception of human meaning to function, but human beings do. Science has been enormously successful without any acknowledgement of human meaning, but human beings cannot live without it. Thus people may be more receptive to science that offers them a sense of purpose. If science can delineate a place for human life that is more than a purely mechanistic and materialistic view of existence and if science can allow for a more humanistic interpretation of the universe, people may find science more approachable. The remarkable creativity of science is an integral part of human culture. Scientists can help bring this about by engaging with society in a wider capacity. I think there needs to be a public relations campaign from the American

Association for the Advancement of Science to show how important science is to humanity—and how important humanity is to science.

The most salient commonality between science and religion is the drive to advance the human enterprise. The *practice* of science is values-neutral, but the *objectives* of science are chockfull of values. Like religion, science promises a collective salvation of humanity. Like religion, science is devoted to the alleviation of human suffering and the advancement of humankind. The time has come to affirm the vital importance of science and religion to humanity and to the planet. It often takes modern science to develop the technology that expands the yield of fertile soil to produce more food. But it also takes the will and motivation of millions of religious people to make sure that the fruit of that technology goes to where it is most needed.

In conclusion: *Knowledge* of the material world and the natural order of things have brought humanity unimaginable wealth and prosperity. Yet what we desire the most is *truth*: understanding our special place in the world; *purpose*: a meaningful personal destiny; and *wisdom*: the guidance to lead a good life. Material knowledge is entirely the province of *science*; truth, purpose, and wisdom are largely the province of *religion*.

# The Dynamics of Faith and Reason

I have often said that atheism requires faith as much as theism. But this characterization goes against the conventional view of the debate, which defines faith purely in religious terms. In fact, the word *faith* is often used as a synonym for religion. "What is your faith?" people ask, by which they mean, "What religious tradition do you practice?" Not only is faith held to be synonymous with religion, but reason is thought to be synonymous with science—and thus the very antithesis of faith.

The more vocal unbelievers live by the assumption that their atheism is based on reason, which implies an outright repudiation of faith. They claim to have rationally considered all the relevant evidence of the debate and concluded that there is no God. But I do not think that atheism is a rational choice any more than I think most believers came to their creed by a rational weighing of available evidence. In almost all instances, this "evidence" was selectively chosen and interpreted. People give reasons for their belief *after the fact* to rationalize and justify what was most assuredly a faith-based decision.

As I will explain further in this chapter, faith has always been a part of science and reason has always been a part of religion. In fact, Christianity allowed reason into theology from the earliest days: God was thought to be the rational creator of a rational universe that was comprehensible to rational humans who were created in the image of the rational God. Thus the world created by God was intelligible to human reason.

One of the most fascinating features of critical reasoning, however, is its capacity to grow spontaneously, and to encompass a broadening scope of inquiry. Questioning begets more questioning. In time, the critical reasoning that was used to know God more fully was also used to throw doubt on the claims of the Catholic Church. As a consequence, Christian reformers established the right to dissent and the free expression of belief. This resulted in a further examination of scripture, which led to additional questions regarding its consistency and infallibility. Increasingly, Christian reformers, whether intentionally or not, encouraged a spirit of critical inquiry that ultimately led to challenging the authority and veracity of the Bible, the Church, and faith itself.

## Three Levels of Debate

The focus of this book has been the debate between believers and unbelievers. But it is important to realize that the debate between theism and atheism points to the concomitant debate between religion and science and, on a deeper level, the tension between faith and reason.

As shown below, two dichotomous trains of thought are widely accepted, especially among hard-core unbelievers: (1) Atheism is based on Science, which is grounded in Reason; and (2) Theism is a form of Religion, which is based on Faith. And the two dimensions are seen as being in constant opposition:

Atheism → Science → Reason

versus

Theism → Religion → Faith

Most people writing about this debate view these two trains of thinking as incompatible at every phase: theism and atheism are in opposition; religion and science are discordant; faith and reason are in conflict. I want to propose another way of understanding these three dyads. They are related, but in a more complex and subtle manner than conventionally described.

- Atheism and theism are mutually exclusive and *contradictory* (one is the direct negation of the other).

- Science and religion can coexist with a minimum of conflict (based on interpretation), and are mainly *complementary*.

- Reason and faith are two dimensions of one truth; they are *interdependent*: both are necessary components of science *and* religion.

When we look at these three dyads, the greatest conflict is between atheism and theism—they are fully incompatible beliefs. As I have already shown in Chapter 9, religion and science are only partially in conflict, depending on the interpretation, but are essentially complementary. Faith and reason are not in conflict; they are mutually *inclusive*; they are two necessary faculties of every belief. Further, science is *not* synonymous with reason and religion is *not* synonymous with faith. Religion has always incorporated reason as well as faith. And science has always required faith as well as reason.

We can summarize as follows: theism and atheism are *competitive beliefs*; religion and science are *complementary truths*; and faith and reason are *essential capacities for truth*.

## Belief = Faith + Reason

The biggest lesson here is that faith and reason are *never* in conflict. They are the warp and woof, the yin and yang of any belief system. In fact, identifying the "reason" part of a belief distinct from the "faith" part is very difficult. When we look at a belief and try to tease out the faith part, we invariably run into reason. And when we try to tease out the reason part, we run into faith. Like protons and neutrons that are both made up of quarks, just different kinds, religion and science are both made up of faith and reason, just different degrees.

Faith and reason are two different faculties to discover one truth, a conception also held by Pope John Paul II: "Faith and reason are like two wings on which the human spirit rises to the contemplation of truth."

## The Search for Truth

A desire to discover *truth* is naturally and spontaneously awakened in humans by the contemplation of creation, specifically the contradiction between who we are (mortal, finite) and who we long to be (eternal, infinite). It is an innate property of reason to ask why things are the way they are and why they are not otherwise. Knowing that things *could have been otherwise* gives rise to our perennial existential questions: Why is there something and not nothing? Where did I come from? Why is there evil? What comes after this life?

The answers to these questions of ultimate concern, to use Paul Tillich's phrase, determine the direction people take in their lives. What's fascinating is that truth-seeking is actually a series of cycles, each one starting with reason (questions) and ending in faith (answers), followed by another round of reason and faith, and still another.

## Two Kinds of Reason

Reason is a process of seeing a contradiction and wanting it resolved; seeing a problem and wanting it solved; seeing a question and wanting it answered. In that context, there are two kinds of reason: *instinctive* and *intentional*.

Instinctive reason functions below the level of consciousness and is always "on"—questioning, seeking, and doubting. Instinctive reason seems to zero in on contradiction, resulting in an uncomfortable intellectual "feeling" known as cognitive dissonance, a term formulated by psychologist Leon Festinger. His theory is that dissonance, being psychologically uncomfortable, motivates a person to try to reduce the dissonance and achieve consonance. "I am proposing," writes Festinger, "that dissonance, the existence of non-fitting relations among cognitions, is a motivating factor in its own right." I would add that dissonance is especially uncomfortable when it involves one's existential beliefs about the self, the world, and God.

Such dissonance motivates us to seek a resolution, which employs the *intentional* form of reason. This is an analytical tool that we can consciously project onto any contradiction or problem we wish to understand. It is the capacity for exploration and examination, rational discourse and critical reasoning, in the search for truth. It is what we use to isolate and rationalize a version of truth that resolves the cognitive dissonance.

## Faith as Fulfillment

Faith is the universal human capacity to address our ultimate concerns. It is a personal orientation that centers us, provides the values that shape our decisions, and goes to the core of our identity. Whether we become believers or nonbelievers, we always use faith to make sense of our lives. Faith pertains to our foundational worldview: whether we think people are trustworthy; whether we believe wealth will make us happy; whether science tells us the truth of reality; whether there is a God. These are the unprovable assumptions that underlie all our acts of reasoning. Facts do not require faith, but the belief systems through which we interpret those facts are based on faith.

Faith is a *trustful surrender,* which is different from blind submission. In faith, we are not giving up our autonomy. We are putting our trust in an ideal that we believe will enhance our life in some way. Faith is more than an act of acquiescence; it is also an act of confidence. But we must remember that we cannot *will* faith; we can only give ourselves to it. Faith is an unconditional embrace.

As the Book of Hebrews (11:1) put it: "Faith is the substance of things hoped for, the evidence of things not seen." Faith is the intuition that one is proceeding in the right direction. It is our conviction that the world is intelligible on our terms, and that truth is worth seeking. Faith is also trust in our own experience and powers of analysis. Even our capacity for reason requires that we have faith in its ability to arrive at the truth.

## Believing: The Cycle of Faith and Reason

Belief, therefore, is not static; it is a dynamic process mediated by the interplay of faith and reason. Faith and reason are not distinct pathways to truth; they are both necessary capacities in the search for and the embrace of one truth (be it religious or secular).

Faith is the solidity upon which we base our lives; reason is the uncertainty that pushes us forward. They make for the constant progression of knowledge. Their dynamism comes not from conflict but from tension, not from competition but from synergy. Reason is searching; faith is embracing. If reason is the source of questions and criticism, faith is the source of certainty and assurance. Reason is freedom-to-be; faith drives us to connect with the source of being.

Militant atheists who want to eliminate faith are misguided. Not only is it not desirable, it is not even possible. We always engage the two capacities at the same time. Reason brings faith to life, making it flexible and self-correcting. Faith gives reason a direction and purpose.

Reason without faith engenders doubt, distrust, and cynicism. Faith without reason becomes absolutist and totalist.

Just as there are unquestioning religious believers, there are also unyielding scientists who never question their own *faith* in reason. And just as there are open-minded scientists, there are also many intrepid religious people who apply *reason* to their faith.

## Faith Is Necessary for Science

Contrary to what atheists want to believe, faith is an inextricable part of science. All scientific inquiry incorporates faith with regard to suppositions about the world and about the scientific method.

The scientist holds foundational assumptions about the validity of the scientific model and the veracity of existing scientific knowledge. All science proceeds from the position that nature is ordered in a rational and intelligible way. A person who thought the universe was a meaningless jumble could not be a scientist. Like the religious faith in an absolute, omniscient God, the scientist has faith that the universe is governed by dependable, immutable, universal mathematical laws. The Dalai Lama offered this concurring observation in his book, *The Universe in a Single Atom:* "The view that all aspects of reality can be reduced to matter and its various particles is, to my mind, as much a metaphysical position as the view that an organizing intelligence created and controls reality." Science and religion presuppose a rational and knowable foundation on which the universe is built, and in both cases that is a matter of faith.

An additional dimension of faith is also expressed in *scientism,* which I previously defined as a belief that the materialist model of reality is all that exists and that science in effect disproves the existence of God. Scientism does not rely on empirically derived evidence for these conclusions, for there can be none. Thus, like religion, it makes claims that cannot be tested or proven. The hallmark of scientism—accepting reason as the only path to truth while at the same time negating faith—paradoxically requires faith.

## Reason Is Required for Healthy Religion

We can clearly see reason at work in healthy religious beliefs on many levels. Reason is employed by theologically oriented people who strive to understand God, despite the fact that God is quintessentially unknowable. We all recognize that the Infinite cannot be explicated, yet over the ages millions of people have devoted a substantial part of their lives trying to do just that. Reason is also present in the often painful process of doubt and self-questioning. Reason further manifests in efforts to defend the belief system from outside challenges as well as in attempts to accommodate those very challenges and evolve the understanding of religion to be consistent with scientific discoveries.

Religious views can be rational when they are structured and elaborated in a critical and reflective way, using criteria that are open to rational interpretation. And one of the Enlightenment's major lessons was that God would prefer the devotion that arises from skeptical inquiry over devotion based on unquestioning acceptance. Although this may be contrary to fundamentalist belief, it is the only way religion can grow and mature.

According to religious scholars, humankind is obliged to use the faculty of reason because it is understood to have been a gift from God that will help to reveal God. As an integral part of religious belief, reason makes possible a self-correcting process, much like science is self-correcting. Critical reasoning may uncover contradictions and imperfections, but that is what makes for a flexible, open-minded religion. Doubt therefore is a part of faith, and skepticism is integral to healthy religious belief.

Many observers through the ages have recognized that the commitment to work through doubt is necessary for a healthy faith. Peter Abelard wrote in *Theologia*, "The first key to wisdom is assiduous and frequent questioning. For by doubting we come to inquiry, and by inquiry we arrive at truth." And Francis Bacon stated in *Advancement of Learning*, "If a man will begin with certainties, he shall end in doubts; but if he will be content to begin with doubts, he shall end in certainties."

For centuries, religious scholars have found some of their most firmly held beliefs challenged by new scientific understanding. The majority of faithful believers responded by restating, reinterpreting, or revising their beliefs as they adapted to new knowledge, from heliocentrism to evolution. It is thus important that religionists not view reason as an enemy of faith. Science should not be seen as weakening faith, but rather as challenging it to become stronger, deeper, and more firmly grounded in truth. Only by challenging traditional assumptions can a person understand what is truly worth believing.

# The Existential Implications of Science: Does Life Have a Purpose?

All this talk about religion and science leads to some highly provoca-tive questions: Is the universe only what science teaches us—a dead place where a small amount of life accidentally developed? Or is life an integral and inevitable part of the physical universe? And what is the place of humanity in the grand scheme of things?

According to a strict interpretation of science, life has no purpose beyond what we bring to it. Nobel physicist Murray Gell-Mann put it poignantly, "Life can perfectly well emerge from the laws of physics plus accidents." And we all realize that there is little inherent meaning in a life that is predicated on randomness and chance.

I am convinced that most unbelievers who accept the scientific narrative about life do not understand the existential implications of this cosmic view. I have found that even the most secular-minded people want to believe that evolution is progressive; that man is the pinnacle of evolutionary development; and that we are above animals in terms of our "gifts"—love and language, consciousness and culture, freedom and faith, mind and morality. The problem is that the scientific explanations concerning the development of life leave humanity completely out of the equation. Most scientists still hold to this dictum by chemist Peter William Atkins: "The question of cosmic purpose is an invented notion, wholly without evidential foundation, and equally dismissible as patently absurd."

As I have also said, the religious narrative's advantage over science is that it explicitly includes man as a central participant in the cosmic drama. In science, however, man is little more than the incidental result of a vast concatenation of unintended events. This is a hugely important distinction. The greatest problem with science is that when we look at the long and fascinating process from the big bang to human evolution, there is nothing special about man—and nothing special about me or you.

The notion that we are just the laws of physics plus accidents has been widely accepted by the scientific community. But almost no layperson, even the most secular among us, accepts that as definitive. Most people believe that there are forces at work in the universe that rise above the purely physical and mechanical laws revealed by science. And this stems not from a pervasive scientific ignorance, but from a deep-seated idea about the nature of life and humanity.

Like the theism-atheism debate, which is assumed to be a simple dichotomy between those who believe and those who don't, the purpose-of-life debate is assumed to be between two interpretations: the creationist view or the scientific view. In the former, humans occupy a special place in the universe created by God; in the latter, humans are the insignificant and unplanned outcome of a process that cares not for our existence.

In this chapter, I want to show that we have a *third* choice. We can remain loyal to the veracity of the scientific narrative of a world without God, while at the same time entertain the suggestion that something more creative may be at work in the physical universe. The fact that the question of life's purpose goes well beyond the limits of scientific knowledge only means this is a philosophical rather than a scientific question. But it is still a question worth asking—even by scientists. The conclusion I will come to is that, although I accept the reality of science totally, I am not sure that science reveals the totality of reality—or ever will.

## Do You Believe Humans Are Special?

The evidence for evolution is overwhelming. Countless fossil discoveries have allowed scientists to trace the evolution of today's organisms from earlier forms. DNA sequencing has confirmed beyond any doubt that all living creatures share a common origin. Innumerable examples of evolution in action can be seen all around us. Evolution is as firmly established a scientific fact as the roundness of Earth.

Yet scientists say one misconception about evolution persists in the popular mind: that it is progressive. We have all seen the graphic depiction of the "ascent of man." In it, we see several hominids walking. The first is a chimpanzee or other primate ancestor ambling on four limbs; followed by a proto-human like *Astralopithecus*; followed by the intermediary forms of our *Homo* species such as *habilis* or *erectus*; then finally modern man, *Homo sapiens*. Modern man is shown as the pinnacle of evolutionary development.

The "ascent of man" graphic suggests that the emergence of humanity was inevitable—like the growing height of a child as he matures from toddler to adult. And who can look at the history of life and not see some form of "progress": greater organization, autonomy, and intelligence? Even among people who claim to embrace evolution and exclude religion, the idea that evolution follows a progressive trajectory is pervasive. This is revealing because it suggests that the strict scientific materialist conception of life is hard to swallow. It goes against our intuition.

However, this progressive conception is widely ridiculed within the scientific community. According to Stephen Jay Gould and other hard-core evolutionists, this graphic depicts something that is far outside Darwinian orthodoxy. Indeed, it is evolutionary heresy. The idea of evolutionary progress so incites scientists because it mirrors the core belief in the major religious traditions that humanity occupies a privileged status in God's creation—that the universe was created with humanity in mind.

Carl Sagan challenged "our posturings, our imagined self-importance, the delusion that we have some privileged position in the universe." Darwin himself mistrusted the idea, having written that "no innate tendency to progressive development exists" in evolution. His theory of natural selection gives no ground for it and does not require it. Natural selection arranged evolving species as a radiating bush rather than a ladder, accounting for all kinds of development. Thus, if you believe there is any progressive tendency in evolution—toward intelligence or complexity or consciousness—you are suggesting teleology and intentionality, which is flatly denied in evolutionary thought.

Most of us still want to believe that we are, if not the center of the universe, then the central living organism on planet Earth, with its 3.5 billion years of evolutionary history—that we are in some way a "special" and "noble" species. Stephen Jay Gould was especially concerned with this misconception and wrote about it extensively: "The vaunted progress of life is really random motion away from simple beginnings, not directed impetus toward inherently advantageous complexity." He has further stated, "We are glorious accidents of an unpredictable process with no drive to complexity, not the expected results of evolutionary principles that yearn to produce a creature capable of understanding the mode of its own necessary construction."

To most everyone's sense of reality, humanity could not have been a cosmic accident. But that is exactly what science is telling us: We are a product of the undirected, purposeless, and random activity of the physical universe.

## Scientific Reductionism

Reductionism, the dominant principle in scientific understanding, says that the explanations for higher-order entities are found in lower-order phenomena. And in its strongest form, reductionism holds that all levels of species complexity can be explained by the underlying laws and forces that govern the interactions of the elementary particles of physics.

According to physicist Steven Weinberg, "All the explanatory arrows point downward, from societies to people, to organs, to cells, to biochemistry, to chemistry, and ultimately to physics." Francis Crick, the Nobel biologist and codiscoverer of DNA, has declared that his work scientifically established that there is no soul or consciousness: "Eventually one may hope to have the whole of biology 'explained' in terms of the level below it, and so on right down to the atomic level. The knowledge we have already makes it highly unlikely that there is anything that cannot be explained by physics and chemistry." We also have Edward O. Wilson, in his book *Consilience*, saying that "all tangible phenomena, from the birth of stars to the workings of social institutions, are based on material processes that are ultimately reducible, however long and tortuous the sequences, to the laws of physics." And evolutionary philosopher Michael Ruse said, "There is no reason to think that biology calls for special life forces over and above the usual processes of physics and chemistry. Nor is there reason to think that biology is little more than complicated physics and chemistry."

Thus, radical reductionism is the view that everything in the universe is made up of something more elementary, which is made up of something more elementary, which is made up of something still more elementary, until the original "something" vanishes into a jumble of unseen quarks and leptons. Arthur Koestler, in his book *Janus*, was especially put off by reductionism in the life sciences. He strenuously objected to such "scientific" reductionism as Freud's sexology, Pavlov's dogs, Skinner's rats, Darwin's finches, and Lorenz's geese, where human behavior was seen mainly as expressions of biological impulses and mechanisms. Throwing his hands up, he says reductionism taken literally would mean that man "could ultimately be defined as consisting of nothing but 90% water and 10% minerals—a statement which is no doubt true, but not very helpful."

Amazingly, if we take the assumptions underlying the standard model of life in the universe to their logical conclusion, *life vanishes*. If all life systems are ultimately explained at the level of subatomic physics, the idea of complexity loses its integrity as something new, since the real explanatory power lies in the lowest common denominator of science. The implication: Since no atom in the human body is "living," and we are made only of atoms, can we be said to be living? The quality of "aliveness" is essentially explained away.

Of course, to any casual observer, even most scientists, this borders on the absurd. But science can't acknowledge much more than this. We know we are alive, and we know that there is far more to our lives than the sum of the parts. But in the standard reductive model, life essentially vanishes. Reductionist biologists take the position that once the basic physical mechanisms operating in a biological organism have been identified, life is explained as "nothing but" the processes of ordinary physics. However, I think it is hard for any observer to believe that, essentially, there is no real difference between living and nonliving systems.

## What Is Life?

We all know intuitively what distinguishes life from nonlife. Nietzsche said life is characterized by a "will to power," by which he meant the impulse to strive, grow, expand, seize, and become predominant. Life is *agency*—adapting to the environment but also actively shaping the environment to its own needs. Borrowing heavily from physicist Paul Davies, I have identified 10 characteristics that distinguish life from nonlife. When we look at these characteristics together, it becomes very difficult to accept that all this is essentially derived from the behavior of subatomic particles.

- **Complexity:** The degree of complexity in even the simplest living organisms far exceeds anything we can find in any physical system. Moreover, the complexity is hierarchical, so that at every level we find a bewildering network of feedback mechanisms and controls.

- **Organization:** Biological complexity is not merely complication. The complexity is organized and harmonized so that the organism functions as an integrated whole.

- **Individuality:** Every living organism is unique, both in form and development. Unlike in physics where one usually studies classes of identical objects (e.g., electrons), organisms are individuals.

- **Emergence:** At each new level of complexity in biology, novel and unexpected qualities appear that cannot be reduced to properties of the component parts.

- **Holism:** A living organism consists of a large number of systems that differ greatly in structure and function (e.g., heart, eyes, brain). Yet the components are integrated so that they behave in a coherent and cooperative manner as part of an overarching "plan."

- **Information Processing:** A living organism is a complex information-processing system. What is organized is precisely information: DNA and molecular biology. This enables an organism to reproduce, conveying the information via genes.

- **Growth and Maturation:** Each living organism lives through a genetically based parabola from birth, through successive states of maturation and senescence, and finally death.

- **Purposeful Behavior:** All organisms exhibit behavior that is directed and purposeful. Universally those purposes are survival and reproduction; with respect to humans, that purpose also encompasses meaningful cultural and symbolic endeavors.

- **Subjectivity:** All organisms have an interior life and subjective experience. Higher organisms also possess some measure of "selfness" expressed as autonomy, free will, self-awareness, and personal identity.

- **Openness:** No living being exists in isolation. All organisms are aware of the world outside them in which they operate. Organisms interact with the environment to achieve a dynamic state of equilibrium.

# Can We Create Something From Nothing?

I think the preceding listing goes a long way to explain the distinctive characteristics of life. However, what science has to say about the origins of life is less than inspiring. Indeed, orthodox science would have us believe that the entire edifice of life—all the complexity, organization, purpose, agency, creativity, growth, subjectivity, and consciousness— is really just physics plus lots of accidents over lots of time. So we have MIT's Marvin Minsky saying, "Everything, including that which happens in our brains, depends on these and only these: A set of fixed, deterministic laws; a purely random set of accidents." And Richard Dawkins agrees: "All appearance to the contrary, the only watchmaker in nature is the blind forces of physics."

## Meet CARL

I have named this scientific materialist's formula for the evolution of life the "standard model," which I identify as follows:

$$\text{Human Life} =$$

$$\text{Laws of Physics} \times$$

$$(\text{Chance} + \text{Accidents} + \text{Randomness} + \text{Luck})$$

$$\times\ 3.5\ \text{Billion Years}$$

Or more simply as:

$$\text{HL} = \text{Ph} \times (\text{CARL}) \times 3.5\text{BY}$$

And after we take out the laws of physics, which, as I will explain, are also a function of pure chance, we are left with just:

$$\text{CARL}$$

That's right—according to conventional science, life is CARL, and nothing more. If you find that difficult to believe, join the club.

This process of becoming human is actually a combination of four intermediate phases, each one of which is entirely dependent upon, for lack of a more appropriate word, randomness. If conventional science is to be believed, we evolved from a level of little more than *nothing* to the human mind entirely through a very long process of random events. The only way humanity is special, according to science, is in terms of probability.

**Phase One:** Random Creation of Multiverses = Our Physical Universe

**Phase Two:** Blind Laws of Physics + Chance = Simple Life

**Phase Three:** Simple Life + Genetic Randomness = Complex Life

**Phase Four:** Complex Life + More Accidents = Mind

What scientists are essentially saying is not only are we the laws of physics plus accidents, but that even the laws of physics as we know them are a result of blind chance. To explain, let me introduce you to the *anthropic principle*, which has been proposed by some scientists as a way to explain how it is that our universe seems perfectly calibrated to accommodate life.

We live in a universe where the numerous constants of physics are astonishingly and exquisitely fine-tuned to allow biological complexity to develop—what some have called the "Goldilocks universe." The English physicist Roger Penrose estimated that the odds against our cosmos arising by chance with its exact constant values is about 1 in $10^{300}$, a figure far larger than the number of atomic particles believed to exist in the universe. Therefore, the anthropic principle poses a problem for mainstream science. It would seem to imply some kind of "design" for life. This problem is solved if there is a random distribution of a multitude of universes, maybe an infinite number of universes, where only some (or perhaps just one) have the correct coordinates that support self-conscious life. So through this idea, science is able to claim that our universe is just one of many in a cosmic crapshoot. This is a radical hypothesis because we can have no direct evidence of other universes. And that just gets us through Phase One of the cosmic evolution of humanity.

Evolution already presupposes something miraculous—life. To realize Phase Two in the above sequence (Blind Laws of Physics + Chance = Simple Life), the physicist Paul Davies suggests that the probability of producing a small virus from Earth's "primordial soup" after a billion years is 1 in 10 to the 2-millionth power, which is greater than the chances of flipping heads on a coin 6 million times in a row. We know that life has purpose (at a minimum, survival and reproduction), but since life arose purely by chance, then that purpose is really a function of chance. And, further, science tells us that it is pure chance that enabled the first simple organism to evolve into a complex human being.

## Chance Alone Is Not Enough

The only conclusion we can draw from the reductionist view of science is that *everything* is a product of chance. Whatever you choose as your foundational "starting point," science says we reached the level of human consciousness purely by chance. Therefore the entire structure of reality is built on CARL. And when we add up the probabilities at each of the four stages of cosmic evolution, even providing for many billions of years, the likelihood that a sentient Bruce Sheiman could have arisen to write this sentence is not 1 in a trillion or 1 in a dectillion (1 followed by 33 zeroes) or even one in a googol (1 followed by 100 zeroes)—but 1 in a near-infinity.

Thus did the laws of physics for our one universe arise by chance (from a multitude of possible universes); the first forms of primitive life developed by chance (arising from primordial soup combinations that resulted from the laws of physics plus accidents); the first complex forms of life developed purely by chance (genetic mutations and envi-ronmental randomness); and humans evolved as a consequence of still more improbable occurrences.

I must again assert that I only believe in natural science and do not believe in God. But even for a secular materialist like me, this strin-gently reductionist conception of cosmic evolution leaves me stone cold. It is as implausible as a God-given miracle. The implication to me is clear: We cannot be the exclusive consequence of CARL; but we also are not the result of a divine mandate. I have to find a middle path that allows for some cosmic creativity without suggesting that there is a spiritual dimension governing this whole process.

All of science points toward an absurd universe wherein the gap between Alpha and Omega is bridged by CARL, which is essentially saying that *something* arose from *nothing*—a conclusion that I cannot accept. I cannot agree with biologist Jacques Monod: "Chance is at the source of every innovation, of all creation in the biosphere. Pure chance, absolutely free but blind, at the very root of the stupendous edifice of evolution: this central concept of modern biology is no longer one among other conceivable hypotheses. It is today the sole conceivable hypothesis, the only one that squares with observed and tested fact." Rather, I agree with astronomer Owen Gingerich: "One can believe that some of the evolutionary pathways are so intricate and so complex as to be hopelessly improbable by the rules of random chance."

The most important question in science is how consciousness emerged from the elementary particles and forces of the incipient uni-verse. Put another way: How did the universe get from the level of par-ticle physics to the level of a scientist contemplating particle physics? Science has presented a remarkable explanation. But I have great dif-ficulty understanding that mind developed out of nonmind by accident;

that purposefulness derived from purposelessness; that complex organization happened from the simple mechanics of subatomic particles. "Accident" is an intellectually incomplete argument. At most, it just reveals what we really do not know.

I think that the universe has properties precisely conducive for the emergence of life because life is built into the system. It makes more sense to my feeble mind that we exist because there is a life imperative present in the universe than that it is all the result of CARL. I am suggesting that we regard life with the same degree of inevitability as any physical law.

## Why Do We Have Complexity?

It seems that science cannot acknowledge a vision for the origin of life without denying the very qualities that make life special. The propensity for matter and energy to self-organize in novel and unpredictable ways is a conspicuous feature of nature; it goes against the law of thermodynamics (entropy) and cannot be explained by the known laws of physics. But according to conventional science, it's all explained by a highly improbable confluence of accidents. And if we happen to take "accidents" out of the life-creation equation, we would be left with *nothing*.

Besides the origin of life from nonliving matter, the other question biologists cannot answer is why complexity evolved at all. Stephen Jay Gould, who did not believe in any progressive tendency in evolution, thought he answered that question by suggesting that it is just an issue of "random diffusion away from a wall of simplicity." What this means is that if life started out really simple and there are random expressions on that simple base, life could not have become more simple; it could only have become more complex. In other words, there was only one direction in which to evolve, and that was to greater complexity.

This sounds plausible, until we give it more thought. One way to measure complexity is in terms of energy, specifically "energy rate density" or energy usage in relation to mass. According to *New Scientist* magazine, "If we look at energy flow in relation to mass, we find a real and impressive trend on increasing energy per time per mass for over 10 billion years of the universe's existence." And, "With few exceptions, energy-flow diagnostics show rising complexity throughout biological evolution. Starting with life's precursor molecules all the way up to plants, animals, brains [and social organizations], the greater the complexity of a system, the greater the flow of energy density through that system, either to build it or maintain it, or both."

It is a cardinal rule of evolution that nature prefers economy and efficiency. Evolutionary philosopher Daniel Dennett said, "The stinginess of nature can be seen everywhere we look." That is why, biologists suggest, cave fish are eyeless and parasitic worms gutless—they had no need for these faculties and they were selected out. And there are many other examples of evolution's affinity for simplicity and efficiency. In that context, life in general and human life in particular are exceptional, even aberrational. Yet it is clear that in the evolutionary sweepstakes, complexity overall offers no advantages and may offer disadvantages compared to simpler versions of life that require less energy.

Why is nature, typically so stingy and economical, so extravagant with higher organisms? In a parsimonious universe where the only imperatives are preservation and procreation, how is complexity even possible? To my mind, in the pure evolutionary process of minimizing expenditures to maximize survival, this conspicuous consumption would be like my building a nuclear power plant merely to heat one home, or buying a jet plane merely to cross the street. They are the opposite of economical frugality. Gould said that evolution could only have grown more complex. That is not true. It could have remained simple. But evolution reveals a general trend to complexity. There are many instances when organisms disappear, go extinct. But where is the evidence for *simplification?* We know that evolution does favor simplicity—bacteria. So there should be innumerable instances of evolution becoming more simple after it had become more complex. But very few examples are known to exist.

Scientists will say that complexity is unintended and accidental, but such an "accident" is like water running up a hill. And the additional mystery is that the complex whole exhibits properties that are not readily explained by understanding those parts. The complex whole often exhibits "emergent" features that are lawful in their own right. The web of life, the most complex system we know of in the universe, violates no laws of physics, yet cannot be reduced to those natural laws and in many ways is lawless and ceaselessly creative.

Regarding the evolution of humans, we can document all of the incremental changes from the beginning. And I have no doubt that evolution has been the medium for every stage in the long and disjointed process of producing a human being. It is the *whole* that I do not understand, rather than the incremental segments. And words like "random" and "unguided" leave me intellectually unsatisfied. I know that randomness is a big part of the process, but by itself it seems terribly inadequate. And it is clear that so long as environmental conditions are amenable, complex life seems at little risk of extinction, almost as if it were "built into" the evolutionary system.

## How Do We Explain Complexity?

A number of thinkers have been asking the same questions: How does life develop from the universe of physical laws? How does life evolve into complex beings able to contemplate their own existence? Nearly a hundred years ago, Nobel laureate and French philosopher Henri Bergson sought to explain evolution as a creative force that keeps pushing upward toward consciousness and intelligence. Bergson's *élan vital* or life force is not seriously considered by many people today, but his idea of "creative evolution" has persisted.

Nobel laureate physicist Erwin Schrodinger went against the Second Law of Thermodynamics (which says that a system tends toward greater disorder) with this dictum: "What an organism feeds on is negative entropy." Negative entropy is the power of living organisms to "build up" rather than to break down, to create complex structures out of simpler elements, and order out of disorder. Luigi Fantappie, a leading Italian mathematician, postulated an opposing law to entropy he called *syntropy*. Syntropic phenomena invert the law of entropy by tending toward order, differentiation, and organization. Fantappie concluded that syntropy is the essence of life: "The law of life is not the law of mechanical causes; this is the law of nonlife, the law of death, the law of entropy; the law which dominates life is the law of syntropy." He stated that syntropy "produces an intelligent process of growth towards forms which are always more complex, organized and evolved." In addition, Nobel laureate Albert Szent-Gyorgyi proposed his own version of syntropy as an "innate drive in living matter to perfect itself."

More recently, several distinguished scientists have identified "emergence" as the tendency within evolution to develop entirely new properties, such as life and consciousness, at certain critical points. Cambridge biologist Simon Conway Morris says that "there is, if you like, seeded into the initiation of the universe itself the inevitability of intelligence." Nobel laureate Christian de Duve, in his book *Vital Dust*, describes the universe as "pregnant with life" and calls life "a cosmic imperative."

The biophysicist Stuart Kauffman declares that we are "at home in the universe," and that life is not just a random by-product of nature, but a fundamental part of the workings of the universe. In his book *Reinventing the Sacred*, Kauffman describes emergence as "the arising of novel and coherent structures, patterns and properties during the process of self-organization in complex systems." Lastly, physicist Paul Davies sees a similar principle or property integral to evolution. In his book, *Cosmic Jackpot*, he says there exists "an organizing principle that facilitates the emergence of biological complexity, fast-tracking matter and energy along the road to life."

These scientists are suggesting that life is implied in matter and complexity is implied in life. The question arises about the nature of the "emergent" principle that suffuses life. It may be tempting to attribute it to a spiritual source, but that is definitely not what I believe. This syntropy or emergence is and has always been a part of the material or natural world. There is no need for a divine source.

Nor is there any need for duality. It is easy to read into this phenomenon a "vital" principle, as Bergson did. But that would be incorrect. Life is a natural emergent property arising when a certain threshold of organization and complexity is attained. This is holism (it is integral to the complexity) and not dualism (a separate vital force). But it is important to note that the collective system possesses a remarkable property (life) not possessed by any of the constituent parts. We can speak of a principle that manifests over and above the known laws of physics, but it does not contradict those laws of physics. It works through them and harnesses them to generate novelty. It is not a separate force but is integral to the physical reality. Paul Davies calls it a "software" principle as opposed to the "hardware" laws that are the traditional subject matter of physics, but it is also compatible with those underlying laws. Davies believes this "software" principle governs the behavior of organization and complexity in nature.

I realize this is all just stating the obvious. But this conception remains profoundly different from what science teaches us. We are acknowledging that life is the product of some intentionality intrinsic to matter rather than being a result of a long sequence of chance, accidents, randomness, and luck. It is an opposing imperative to reductionism that I call *accretionism:* a process of bottom-up assembling, integrating, and self-organizing that, given hospitable circumstances, of necessity results in biological and behavioral complexity.

The obvious reality is that life consists of irreducible complexity. Many orthodox scientists will counterclaim that life is certainly reducible, but then these scientists need to show me how we can build life from the bottom up with just the laws of physics plus accidents. That is what is unbelievable. There must be an "innate force" within all living matter that functions to build up and integrate an organism. But rather than explaining how life emerged, evolutionary scientists take the easy way out by presupposing the existence of life and *assuming* it all works backward to the laws of physics (plus accidents).

My conception does not in any way contradict evolution or suggest any divine principle. But it does require revising our understanding of evolution. Stuart Kauffman said, "It is not that Darwin is wrong, but that he got hold of only part of the truth. It is this single-force view that I believe is inadequate, for it fails to notice, fails to stress, fails to incorporate the possibility that simple and complex systems exhibit order spontaneously." We must conclude that life is written in the laws of the universe, and complexity in the laws of life.

## Life Is Purposeful

I am finally coming to understand that it is not possible for a purposeless universe to produce purposeful beings. Therefore, I must assume the universal presence of purpose throughout evolution. The question remains: Is our purpose only to survive and reproduce our genes? If that were all life is about, it would not seem that life has much intrinsic meaning. And where does this need for gene reproduction come from? Nothing gives me a Sisyphusian feeling more than to think that all I and my progeny are about is the replication of the same genes. Have we given any thought to how absurd it seems to reproduce for the sake of more reproduction?

I have a novel approach to the purpose question. Rather than thinking that all our behavior and culture are in the service of the twin evolutionary imperatives of preservation and procreation, I have reversed the question to ask whether survival and reproduction are themselves in the service of a more meaningful imperative. What if our selfish genes are supporting a *higher* purpose, but since science can only see and measure the drive for genetic replication, it assumes that is what the whole evolutionary enterprise is all about?

My argument is simple: Rather than assuming that consciousness is reducible to brain activity, which is reducible to chemistry and physics, why not assume that the physics and chemistry and brain activity are in the service of something like consciousness?

I admit that I am pushing a romantic view of cosmic evolution, which has been described by several prominent scientists. Here is Christian de Duve: "Life and mind emerge not as freakish accidents, but as natural manifestations of matter, written into the fabric of the universe. I view this universe not as a 'cosmic joke,' but as a meaningful entity—made in such a way as to generate life and mind, bound to give birth to thinking beings able to discern truth, apprehend beauty, feel love, yearn for goodness, and experience mystery."

The purpose of the universe is for it to contemplate itself through the self-awareness of humanity. Nature is a structure that allows for the development of self-reflecting, autonomous agents, not purely by accident but partially by intrinsic intention. This is a more fully defined formulation of evolution, albeit with a component that may not be within the narrow realm of scientific inquiry. But the conception assumes that so long as we are here, we know that we are in some sense part of the "plan" where the universe was pregnant with life and life was pregnant with intelligence and consciousness. Physicist Freeman Dyson said, "The more I examine the universe and study the details of its architecture, the more evidence I find that the universe in some sense must have known we were coming."

Chance still plays a big role. And I think that Gould was correct when he wrote, "Wind back the tape of life to the early days of the Burgess Shale [530 million years ago], let it play from an identical starting point, and the chance becomes vanishingly small that anything like human intelligence would grace the replay." Nothing in evolution is predetermined or inevitable. Living organisms are not realized by final causes, in the Aristotelian sense. There is no specific end-goal encoded in the principles of self-organization, only a general trend toward the sort of complex states that are likely to lead to sentient life.

What this says is that I am a part of the cosmic narrative, which has as its purpose the creation of conscious, autonomous beings—something very much like me (and you). The universe "intended" for me to exist—contingent, of course, on amenable conditions that might allow for human development (and it really is contingent: without the asteroid that killed off the dinosaurs 65 million years ago, humanity could not today exist). This is certainly anthropocentric; indeed, it is *ego*-centric, for it says that evolution has a purpose and it matches my purpose to exist—and your purpose, too.

Recognize that I am not suggesting anything grandiose: no Eternal Mind realizing itself through nature; no Absolute Spirit becoming self-aware through human history; no transcendent Omega Point that the universe will converge upon; no Supreme Spiritual Reality directing the universe toward an apotheosis that is man; no grand destiny for humankind—these are all beautiful ideas, and I would love to believe in any one of them. But I do not.

On the other hand, I am not about to succumb to the idea that CARL (chance, accidents, randomness, and luck) is all that life and the universe are about. This is my effort to snatch a little meaning and purpose from the meaningless mechanics of scientific materialism. It tells me that while I do not believe in God, my being has a place in the scheme of things. For me, the most fascinating conception is as Davies says: "Somehow, the universe has engineered its own self-awareness." It means that we are *more* than simple life forms; we are *more* than randomness; we are *more* than mechanical and blind forces. I am searching for an explanation that gives me a cosmic reason to sit at my desk and write these words.

All of this is still of the material world, but it also enables us to rise above the materiality of this world by creating some new "stuff"— culture, consciousness, morality, selfness, intelligence. To believe in purpose is to believe that consciousness is a new level of existence, not just a manifestation of biological laws that are a manifestation of chemical laws that are a manifestation of physical laws—and all that differs from one level to the other is some implausible confluence of "accidents."

We can derive a small amount of meaning in knowing that we are not an "accident," but rather part of a process that in one sense intends to create our very existence. As astronomer Owen Gingerich said, "I am psychologically incapable of believing that the universe is meaningless. I believe the universe has a purpose, and our greatest intellectual challenge as human beings is to glimpse what this purpose might be. Quite possibly, the purpose of the universe is to provide a congenial home for self-conscious creatures who can ask profound questions and who can probe the nature of the universe itself."

## No Creator Necessary

Because I do not believe that the scientific explanation for the origin of life as it is currently defined tells the entire story does not mean that I accept the alternative that it must therefore be the creation of God. So I do not agree with Christian scholar Paul Copan who stated, "The better unifying explanation is a supremely valuable, supremely aware, reasoning, truthful, powerful, intelligent, beautiful being." I think that is a huge leap of faith that I am unable to justify.

Thus, I am here proposing a Third Way of understanding the purpose of life in the universe. Following is a simple matrix to help explain the Third Way. The dimensions down the left reflect the dichotomy of origins: either a divine creation of the world or a natural origin. The dimensions on the top reflect the two options of a purposeful and purposeless universe.

|  | **Purposeful Universe** | **Purposeless Universe** |
|---|---|---|
| **Divine Origin** | Biblical Creationist | N/A |
| **Natural Origin** | *Third Way* | Scientific Materialist |

The matrix gives us four scenarios, of which only three are viable for the purpose of this discussion:

1. A universe with a divine origin is by definition purposeful. This is the conception held by biblical creationists; I also put into this category believers who accept evolution because they still hold that the world has a divine origin.

2. The universe conceived by the scientific materialist is unwavering in the conviction that the universe not only has a natural origin but is also devoid of any purpose, intentionality, or creativity; everything is a function of randomness, accidents, and chance.

3. The Third Way affirms that the universe has a natural origin and contains nothing immaterial; however, this conception holds that the universe does possess an intrinsic purposefulness that is as much a part of evolution as is natural selection.

For me the question is whether the essential properties of life require a Transcendent Spiritual Reality. And I am saying *they do not*. What confounds me is why some scientists actively reject any purpose inherent in the process of life; why they seem so hard-pressed to deny the extra dimension that makes life *alive*. The reason, I surmise, is that by not fitting into the standard paradigm, the default conclusion is that the process of life is outside the realm of the material world. That would be true only if we assume that the material world is just what is revealed by reductionist science. And that is where I and these scientists disagree. It is possible for the biophilic properties of the universe to be wholly within the material world, not outside it—despite the inability of the scientific method to affirm its identity. It is a matter of recognizing that while science only reveals the material world, not every aspect of the material world can be revealed by science.

Most atheists would no doubt like a universe with God if only we could believe in God. But we are atheists, after all, so I see no way to shoehorn God into the process. In the end, if we cannot believe in God, we are left with the scientific conception of life, which leaves little allowance for intrinsic meaning. It is true that we can use our free will to create our own meaning. But, first, you have to believe that we actually have free will, something that science increasingly is placing in doubt.

So for most of us, we need a source of meaning that is more than our own or even our culture's conception of meaning. Cultural observer and atheist Theodore Dalrymple said much the same: "However many times philosophers say that it is up to ourselves, and to no one else, to find the meaning of life, we continue to long for a transcendent purpose immanent in existence itself, independent of our own wills." To accomplish this, however, we need to revise our understanding of the nature of the physical world to include a *life imperative*.

## Design without a Designer

A cosmic designer does not offer anything to me that a self-generative universe cannot. I have always had the question in the back of my mind that "If God created the world, what created God?" Certainly, if God can be said to have always existed or is self-created, then the universe can be said to have always existed in some form or was self-created. Thus, to claim that design requires a designer as a watch requires a watchmaker does not seem to be defensible. I am satisfied to accept that the universe is self-contained.

The most super-charged word in this debate is "design." To most people in the debate, design implies a designer. And this is unfortunate because my definition of design is more like this one I found: "A basic scheme or pattern that affects and controls function or development." Thus something that exhibits the characteristics of design need not have a designer. I believe this notion of "designer" results from anthropomorphism.

For me, life definitely exhibits "design" because it exhibits a *complex organization that follows laws and rules for the purpose of survival and reproduction—and possibly higher functions like consciousness and subjective experience.* Life shows complexity, structure, order, and organization— thus, all life exhibits design in a manner of speaking. This is hard to deny, but because of this automatic association of design with designer, scientists have no choice but to deny design. I want to affirm here that we can have intelligent design *without* intelligence divine.

The problem with the issue as it now stands is that design is inextricably linked with creationism, where the acceptance of evolution implies that one rejects creationism *and* design. But there is a middle path. I accept natural selection as fact, but I am not convinced it explains all that is going on in evolution. Within this conceptualization, I can embrace evolution and reject creationism, but still postulate that something more generative is at work, something like design but without the need for a designer.

I am dissatisfied with the scientific explanation for our universe. Science does not offer an intellectually or emotionally satisfying explanation for:

1. The enormously improbable configuration of a universe capable of supporting life.
2. The emergence of life, even the first single-celled organism.
3. The development of complex life and human consciousness.

Throughout this book I have argued for a Third Way, a compromise path between two polar opposites. The universe displays *intelligence,* but there is no Higher Intelligence. The universe displays *creativity,* but there is no Creator God. The universe displays *design,* but there is no Great Designer. The universe displays *purpose* and *organized complexity,* but there is no Supreme Being behind it.

Paul Davies has written, "Thus although we are not at the center of the universe, human existence does have a powerful wider significance. Whatever the universe as a whole may be about, the scientific evidence suggests that we, in some way, are an integral part of its purpose." All of which leads me to conclude that we are members of a universe of ceaseless creativity in which life, agency, meaning, value, consciousness, and the richness of human experience have a place. Maybe we are special after all, but not in the way religion intended. Even without God, I think it is possible to understand the universe in a way that acknowledges human existence, and, by extension, our own existence.

# Epilogue: Religion Flourishes; Atheism Flounders

*An Atheist Defends Religion* was borne out of a response to the most vociferous proponents of atheism, whose recent books dominated the best-seller lists. I was not alone: in the past five years about 20 books by mainstream believers have been published in response to militant atheism. But I was disappointed because all of them were predictable, one-sided countercritiques of atheism. If I accomplish just one thing in this book, my goal is to show that none of the issues pertaining to religion—science, fundamentalism, politics, atheism, morality, faith—is as simple and straightforward as many commentators have made them out to be. As an atheist who is sympathetic to theism, I have tried to navigate a middle path.

## What Can Take the Place of Religion?

By now we should understand why religion is so integral to human nature and culture. Religion incorporates many expressions of mental health—from community-building to enduring values, from moral behavior to a transcendent sense of purpose. Religion helps people to cope with many of life's greatest questions, dilemmas, and challenges.

One has to ask, therefore, what militant atheists are thinking when they propose to eliminate religion from the lives of six billion people. Religion is so deeply integrated into the behavior of every devout person, it is such a vital unifying system, that supplanting religion would appear to be impossible and undesirable, if not an act of great cruelty.

Many years ago I was among the atheists who thought that religion was coming to an end. Yes, there has been a surge in religious sentiment in the United States, but I believed that the developed world at some point would abandon religion for a purely scientific conception of the universe.

Science, however, fails as a creed for the masses precisely because it lacks *humanity*. As my analysis in this book has shown, for all its wonders, science cannot be made into an ideology capable of replacing religion. It leaves too many existential blanks to be filled by something else—notably, religion. Atheists are certainly correct that science is important to humankind, but science by itself does not build hospitals, console the sick, or succor the poor. In no conceivable permutation is atheism capable of speaking to our heart or our spirit. So long as religion innovates, I believe it will always metamorphose into something that the majority of people will adopt as the primary cultural institution capable of fulfilling many of humanity's most important emotional, moral, and psychological needs.

## Atheism In Crisis

Surveys consistently reveal that only about 1 percent of Americans actually identify themselves as unbelievers, which is no doubt a significant understatement. Few people openly admit to being atheists because that label is also a stigma. It is said that more Americans mistrust atheists than any other group. So it is expected that many unbelievers are "in the closet."

The most ardent proponents of atheism, however, would have us believe that as much as 16 percent of the population consists of unbelievers. That figure was derived from a 2008 study by the Pew Forum on Religion and Public Life entitled, "The U.S. Religious Landscape Survey," wherein 16 percent of Americans identified themselves as "unaffiliated." To claim that all or most of these people are unbelievers is an enormous leap without supporting evidence. In fact, a more recent installment of the same study revealed that 70 percent of the so-called unaffiliated actually believe in God. By calling themselves unaffiliated, these people may be rejecting organized and institutionalized religion, but clearly they are not all rejecting God. When we do the math (the 30 percent who do not believe in God among the 16 percent who are unaffiliated), we arrive at an atheist (including agnostic) estimate of 4.8 percent of the population, which is consistent with decades of Gallup surveys showing that 95 percent of Americans believe in some form of God.

Even at 5 percent, the proportion of Americans who are atheistic or agnostic is very small, which invariably leads secularists to the question: What happened? It has been a hallmark of progressive thought since the Enlightenment that modernity would dispense with religion. With the reign of science, we were all supposed to be atheists by now. Unbelievers are perplexed and disappointed that the theistic "mutation" has flourished, when in fact they should be pleased that social Darwinism has indeed spoken the last word: For the majority, atheism does not work; religion does. According to the *Economist*, the proportion of people attached to the world's four biggest religions—Christianity, Islam, Buddhism, and Hinduism—rose from 67 percent in 1900 to 73 percent in 2005 and may reach 80 percent by 2050.

The reality is that America is in a *secular* crisis. It is the secular ideologies—from Marxism to Freudianism—that have come and gone.

It is the secular paradigms that the majority of people find unsatisfying. And atheism in particular has proven to be a marginal belief. When atheists attempt to come together for some political cause vis-à-vis religionists, typically just a few hundred people show up compared to their theistic opponents, who are able to marshal millions of devotees, suggesting again that atheism may be succumbing to the very fate— irrelevance—that unbelievers once predicted would overtake religion.

The cultural observer Richard Shweder aptly summed up atheism's predicament: "If religion is a delusion, it is a delusion with a future." And columnist David Brooks concurs: "Secularism is not the future; it is yesterday's incorrect vision of the future."

## Lessons for Militant Atheists

I think militant atheism deserves three criticisms with respect to its treatment of science.

### Unfair Comparison of Science and Religion

Militant atheists like Dawkins, Hitchens, and Harris go to great lengths in their books to relegate religion to the lowest cultural status while placing reason and science well above it. However, when atheists criticize the actions of religion, they hold it to much *higher* moral standards than they do science.

Atheists persistently present the realm of science as apart from the selfish inclinations of individuals, the venal profit motives of organizations, and the political interference that has produced such evils as weapons of mass destruction. They portray science in idealized terms, untainted by commercial interests, political intrusions, and ethical conundrums. But when militant atheists portray religion, they critique every political and organizational misdeed that can be attributed to it. Militant atheists speak of organized religion, but not, correspondingly, of *organized science*.

To be fair, militant atheists need to view religion in the same sanitized way as they view science—or understand science through the same lens of doubt and skepticism as they view religion.

## Atheists Debase Science

Militant unbelievers attempt a polemical subterfuge by drawing an association between atheism and science, whereby they claim atheism is justified by a natural-science evaluation of theistic belief.

Science is intrinsically agnostic toward religion; it neither confirms nor denies the existence of God. However, when militant atheists commandeer the "verifiable evidence" orientation of science to justify their unbelief, they are debasing science. When atheists make science into a competing ideology—what I have called scientism—they are exploiting science. Such an effort infuses science with a bias aimed to refute religion and uphold atheism—a distortion not compatible with the values-neutral mission of science.

## The Biggest Loser: Science

In the seemingly interminable debate between religion and science, it is becoming clear to me that the biggest loser is science. There is no substantial religious crisis in America; a large proportion of people are happily religious. The discipline with the most to lose in this competition is science, for two reasons. First, science is the realm least accessible to most Americans. Second, science does not go to the heart of a person's identity the way religion does. Consequently, in a conflict where people are pressured to embrace one realm and repudiate the other, science is usually the discipline that is sacrificed.

Because of my love of science, I find this outcome terribly unfortunate. But to the extent that militant atheists misappropriate science for their own ends, science will continue to suffer from a pervasive public relations problem.

For more commentary, readers are invited to visit
AnAtheistDefendsReligion.com, and you can direct your feedback
to Bruce@AnAtheistDefendsReligion.com. I look forward to receiving
your insights and comments.

# Bibliography

Adorno, T. W., E. Frenkel-Brunswik, D. J. Levinson, and R. N. Sanford. *The Authoritarian Personality*. New York: Harper & Brothers, 1950.

Ali, A. H. "Islam's Silent Moderates." *The New York Times* op-ed, Dec. 7, 2007.

Altizer, T. J. *Mircea Eliade and the Dialectic of the Sacred*. Philadelphia: The Westminster Press, 1963.

American Humanist Association. "Humanist Manifesto III."

Archibold, R. C. "Facing Trial under Terror Law, Radical Claims a New Outlook." *The New York Times*, May 3, 2007.

Armstrong, K. *A Short History of Myth*. Edinburgh: Canongate, 2005.

Baker, A. "The Jihadi Next Door," review of Marc Sageman's *Leaderless Jihad* in *Time*, March 31, 2008.

Barbour, I. G. *Religion and Science: Historical and Contemporary Issues*. Harper San Francisco, 1997.

Barkan, S. E., and L. L. Snowden. *Collective Violence*. Boston: Allyn and Bacon, 2001.

Beauregard, M., and D. O'Leary. *The Spiritual Brain: A Neuroscientist's Case for the Existence of the Soul*. New York: Harper One, 2007.

Becker, E. *The Denial of Death*. New York: Free Press, 1973.

———. *Escape from Evil*. New York: Free Press, 1975.

Benedict, R. *Patterns of Culture*. Cambridge: Houghton Mifflin Co., 1959.

Benedict XVI (Pope). Speech about human rights presented before the United Nations General Assembly, April 18, 2008.

Benson, H., and M. Stark. *Timeless Healing: The Power and Biology of Belief*. New York: Scribner, 1996.

Bergson, H. *Creative Evolution*. New York: Henry Holt and Co., 1911.

Berlinski, D. *The Devil's Delusion: Atheism and Its Scientific Pretensions*. New York: Crown Forum, 2008.

Best, S. "Philosophy Under Fire: The Peter Singer Controversy." DrSteveBest.org.

Bierlein, J. F. *Parallel Myths*. New York: Ballantine Books, 1994.

Blair, T. Speech to launch the Tony Blair Faith Foundation, May 30, 2008, in New York.

Bloom, P. "Is God an Accident?" *The Atlantic Monthly*, Dec. 2005.

Boorstin, D. J. *The Discoverers: A History of Man's Search to Know His World and Himself.* New York: Random House, 1983.

Boyer, P. *Religion Explained: The Evolutionary Origins of Religious Thought.* New York: Basic Books, 2001.

Brennan, B. P. *The Ethics of William James.* New York: Bookman Associates, 1962.

Brooks, A. C. "The Ennui of Saint Teresa." *The Wall Street Journal* op-ed, Sept. 25, 2007.

———. *Gross National Happiness: Why Happiness Matters for America.* New York: Basic Books, 2008.

———. "The Politics of Happiness." *The Wall Street Journal* op-ed, May 21, 2007.

———. "Religious Faith and Charitable Giving." *Policy Review*, October 2003.

———. *Who Really Cares: America's Charity Divide; Who Gives, Who Doesn't, and Why It Matters.* New York: Basic Books, 2006.

Brooks, D. "Kicking the Secularist Habit." *The Atlantic Monthly*, March 2003.

Buber, M., and W. Kaufmann (trans). *I and Thou.* New York: Charles Scribner's Sons, 1970.

Budge, W. *Egyptian Religion.* New York: Bell Publishing, 1959 (1900).

Bunting, M. "The New Atheists Loathe Religion Far Too Much to Plausibly Challenge It." *The Guardian* (UK), May 7, 2007. "The New Tyranny" *The Guardian*, May 25, 2007.

Cahill, T. "The Peaceful Crusader." *The New York Times* op-ed, Dec. 25, 2006.

Caputo, P. *A Rumor of War.* New York: Ballantine Books, 1977.

Carroll, V., and D. Shiflett. *Christianity on Trial: Arguments Against Anti-Religious Bigotry.* San Francisco: Encounter Books, 2002.

Chaisson, E. "The Great Unifier." *New Scientist*, Jan. 7, 2006.

Clark, A., and O. Lelkes. "Religion Linked to Happy Life." BBC News, March 18, 2008.

Clausen, C. "America's Design for Tolerance." *Wilson Quarterly*, Winter 2007.

Cohen, P. "Investigating Links Between Personality and Politics." *The New York Times*, Feb. 12, 2007.

Coleman, R. J. *Competing Truths: Theology and Science as Sibling Rivals.* Harrisburg, PA: Trinity Press International, 2001.

Collins, F. S. *The Language of God: A Scientist Presents Evidence for Belief.* New York: Free Press, 2006.

Collins, F., and S. Weinberg. "Science versus Religion." Debate excerpts available at thebatt.com (Texas A&M).

Copleston, F. *Religion and the One: Philosophies East and West*. London: Search Press, 1982.

Crick, F. *The Astonishing Hypothesis: The Scientific Search for the Soul*. New York: Scribner, 1995.

———. *Of Molecules and Men*. Seattle: University of Washington Press, 1966.

D'Souza, D. "Atheism and Child Murder." DineshDSouza.com, May 9, 2008.

———. *What's So Great About Christianity*. Washington, D.C.: Regnery Publishing, 2007.

Dalai Lama. *The Meaning of Life*. Boston: Wisdom Publications, 2000.

———. *The Universe in a Single Atom*. New York: Morgan Road Books, 2005.

Dalrymple, T. (Anthony Daniels). "What the New Atheists Don't See." *City Journal*, Autumn 2007.

Davies, P. *Cosmic Jackpot: Why Our Universe Is Just Right for Life*. Boston: Houghton Mifflin Co., 2007.

———. *The Fifth Miracle: The Search for the Origin and Meaning of Life*. New York: Simon & Schuster, 1999.

———. *The Mind of God: The Scientific Basis for a Rational World*. New York: Simon & Schuster, 1992.

———. Templeton Prize Address, 1995.

Dawkins, R. "The Atheist." Interview by Gordy Slack on Salon.com April 28, 2005.

———. *The Blind Watchmaker: Why the Evidence of Evolution Reveals a Universe without Design*. New York: W.W. Norton, 1987.

———. "Epiphanies." Selected quotes by Dawkins on *Foreign Policy Online*.

———. "The Flying Spaghetti Monster." Interview by Steve Paulson on Salon.com, Oct. 13, 2006.

———. *The God Delusion*. Boston: Houghton Mifflin Co., 2006.

———. "I Want to Change People's Minds." Interview in *Financial Times* Dec. 16, 2006.

———. "The Illusion of Design." *Natural History,* Nov. 2005.

———. "Is Science a Religion?" *The Humanist,* Jan/Feb. 1997.

———. "Religion: For Dummies." Interview by Laura Sheahen on BeliefNet.com.

———. *River Out of Eden*. New York: Harper Collins, 1995.

———. Transcript of television interview by Sheena McDonald, Aug. 15, 1994.

———. *Unweaving the Rainbow: Science, Delusion and the Appetite for Wonder*. Boston: Houghton Mifflin Co., 1998.

————. "What Good Is Religion?" BeliefNet.com.

————. "Why There Almost Certainly Is No God." Edge.org, Oct. 26, 2006.

Dawkins, R., and S. Pinker. "Is Science Killing the Soul?" Conversation moderated by Tim Radford on Edge.org.

Day, V. *The Irrational Atheist: Dissecting the Unholy Trinity of Dawkins, Harris and Hitchens.* Dallas: Benbella, 2008.

De Duve, C. *Vital Dust: Life as a Cosmic Imperative.* New York: Basic Books, 1995.

Deem, R. "Scientific Studies that Show a Positive Effect of Religion on Health." GodandScience.org.

Dennett, D. C. *Breaking the Spell: Religion as a Natural Phenomenon.* New York: Viking, 2006.

————. "The Evaporation of the Powerful Mystique of Religion." Edge.org, Jan. 5, 2008.

————. "The Harsh Light of Science: Why a Scientific Study of Religion is Necessary." *Seed*, Feb/March 2006.

Di Corpo, U. "Syntropy: A Third Possibility in the Debate on Evolution." Sintropia.it.

Dowd, M. *Thank God for Evolution!: How the Marriage of Science and Religion Will Transform Your Life and Our World.* San Francisco: Council Oak Books, 2007.

Duerlinger, J. (ed). *God: Ultimate Reality and Spiritual Discipline.* New York: Paragon House Publishers, 1984.

Duke University Center for Spirituality, Theology and Health. "Religion and Health: Effects, Mechanisms and Interpretations." March 19, 2007.

Durkheim, E., and K. E. Fields (trans). *The Elementary Forms of Religious Life.* New York: Free Press, 1995 (1912).

Dyson, F. *Disturbing the Universe.* New York: Harper & Row Publishers, 1979.

————. "Progress in Religion." Templeton Prize Address, May 16, 2000. Edge.org.

Eagleton, T. "Lunging, Flailing, Mispunching," review of *The God Delusion* in *London Review of Books*, Oct. 19, 2006.

Easterbrook, G. *Beside Still Waters: Searching for Meaning in an Age of Doubt.* New York: William Morrow & Co., 1998.

*Economist.* Special Report: "The New Religion Wars." Nov. 3, 2007.

————. "Where Angels No Longer Fear to Tread." March 22, 2008.

Eliade, M. *Images and Symbols: Studies in Religious Symbolism.* New York: Sheed & Ward, 1952.

————. *Myth and Reality.* New York: Harper & Row Publishers, 1963.

———. *The Myth of the Eternal Return*. New York: Pantheon Books, 1954.

———. *Myths, Dreams and Mysteries*. New York: Harper & Brothers, 1960.

———. *Myths, Rites, Symbols: A Mircea Eliade Reader*. New York: Harper Colophon Books, 1976.

———. *Rites and Symbols of Initiation: The Mysteries of Birth and Rebirth*. New York: Harper & Row Publishers, 1958.

———. *The Sacred and the Profane*. New York: Harcourt, Brace & World, 1959.

Emmons, R. A. *The Psychology of Ultimate Concerns: Motivation and Spirituality in Personality*. New York: The Guilford Press, 1999.

Festinger, L. *A Theory of Cognitive Dissonance*. Stanford: Stanford University Press, 1957.

Fidler, S. "From Alienation to Annihilation" (motivations for terrorism). *Financial Times,* July 7, 2007.

Findlay, J. N. *Ascent to the Absolute: Metaphysical Papers and Lectures*. London: George Allen & Unwin Ltd., 1970.

Flew, A., and R. A. Varghese. *There Is a God: How the World's Most Notorious Atheist Changed His Mind*. New York: Harper One, 2007.

Gazzaniga, M. S. *The Ethical Brain: The Science of Our Moral Dilemmas*. New York: Harper Perennial, 2006.

Ghosh, A. "Inside the Mind of an Iraqi Suicide Bomber." *Time,* July 4, 2005.

Gibberd, B. "To the Ramparts (Gently)." *The New York Times,* March 23, 2008.

Giles, J. "Born that Way." *New Scientist,* Feb. 2, 2008.

Gingerich, O. *God's Universe*. Cambridge: Belknap Press of Harvard University Press, 2006.

Goldhammer, J. D. *Under the Influence: The Destructive Effects of Group Dynamics*. Amherst, NY: Prometheus Books, 1996.

Gottlieb, A. "Atheists with Attitude." *The New Yorker,* May 21, 2007.

Gould, S. J. "The Evolution of Life on Earth." *Scientific American,* Oct. 1994.

———. *Rocks of Ages: Science and Religion in the Fullness of Life*. New York: Ballantine Publishing Group, 1999.

Greene, B. "Put a Little Science in Your Life." *The New York Times* op-ed, June 1, 2008.

Grigoriadis, V. "The Rise and Fall of the Eco-Radical Underground." *Rolling Stone,* July 28, 2006.

Guengerich, G. "The Heart of Our Faith." *UU World,* Spring 2007.

Haidt, J. "Moral Psychology and the Misunderstanding of Religion." Edge.org.

Haldane, J. *An Intelligent Person's Guide to Religion*. London: Duckworth Overlook, 2005.

Hamer, D. *The God Gene: How Faith Is Hardwired into Our Genes*. New York: Doubleday, 2004.

Hardin, R. *One for All: The Logic of Group Conflict*. Princeton: Princeton University Press, 1995.

Harris, S. *The End of Faith: Religion, Terror and the Future of Reason*. New York: W.W. Norton & Co., 2004.

———. *Letter to a Christian Nation*. New York: Alfred A. Knopf, 2006.

———. "10 Myths—and 10 Truths—About Atheism." Edge.org.

Harris, S., and R. Warren. Debate in *Newsweek*, April 9, 2007.

Hasan, K. "Terrorism Less to Do with Religion than Politics: Sageman." *Daily Times* (Pakistan), June 18, 2008.

Haught, J. A. *Honest Doubt: Essays on Atheism in a Believing Society*. Amherst, NY: Prometheus Books, 2007.

Haught, J. F. *God and the New Atheism*. Louisville: Westminster John Knox Press, 2008.

Hauser, M. D. "The *Discover* Interview (Marc Hauser): Is Morality Innate and Universal?" *Discover*, May 2007.

———. *Moral Minds: How Nature Designed Our Universal Sense of Right and Wrong*. New York: HarperCollins Publishers, 2006.

Hedges, C. *I Don't Believe in Atheists*. New York: Free Press, 2008.

Henig, R. M. "Darwin's God." *The New York Times Magazine*, March 4, 2007.

Hentoff, N. "A Professor of Infanticide at Princeton." *Jewish World Review*, Sept. 13, 1999.

Higgins, A. "Anti-Americans on the March." *The Wall Street Journal*, Dec. 9-10, 2006.

Hitchens, C. *God Is Not Great*. New York: Twelve Books, 2007.

Hocart, A. M. *The Life-Giving Myth and Other Essays*. New York: Grove Press, 1955.

Hood, R. W., P. C. Hill, and W. P. Williamson. *The Psychology of Religious Fundamentalism*. New York: The Guilford Press, 2005.

Horgan, J. "The God Experiments." *Discover*, Nov. 2006.

Hummer, R. A., et al. "Religious Involvement and U.S. Adult Mortality." *Demography*, May 1999.

Humphrey, N. *Soul Searching: Human Nature and Supernatural Belief*. London: Chatto & Windus, 1995.

Huxley. A. *The Perennial Philosophy*. New York: Harper & Brothers Publishers, 1945.

Idler, E., and S. Kasl. "New Research Finds Link Between Religion and Health in Elderly." *Science Daily*, Nov. 1, 1997.

James, W. *Essays on Faith and Morals*. New York: Longmans, Green and Co., 1947.

———. *The Varieties of Religious Experience*. New York: Book-of-the-Month Club, 1997.

———. *The Will to Believe and Other Essays in Popular Philosophy*. Cambridge: Harvard University Press, 1979 (1897).

Janis, I. L. *Victims of Groupthink: A Psychological Study of Foreign-Policy Decisions and Fiascoes*. Boston: Houghton Mifflin Co., 1972.

John Templeton Foundation. "Has Science Made Belief in God Obsolete?" and "Does the Universe Have a Purpose?" Templeton.org.

Johnson, G. "Free-for-All Debate on Science and Religion." *The New York Times*, Nov 21, 2006.

Johnson, J. "A Creed of 'Loathe Thy Neighbor'." *Financial Times*, March 31, 2007.

Jones, D. "The Emerging Moral Psychology." *Prospect*, April 2008.

Jones, N. "Religion and Health: A Dose of Spirituality Can Be Good for Your Body." *Vibrant Life*, Jan. 2004.

Judson, O. "The Selfless Gene." *The Atlantic*, Oct. 2007.

Jung, C. G. *Flying Saucers: A Modern Myth of Things Seen in the Skies*. New York: MJF Books, 1978 (1964).

Kauffman, S. *At Home In the Universe: The Search for the Laws of Self-Organization and Complexity*. New York: Oxford University Press, 1995.

———. "Beyond Reductionism." Edge.org, Nov. 13, 2006.

———. *Reinventing the Sacred: A New View of Science, Reason and Religion*. New York: Basic Books, 2008.

Kecmanovic, D. *The Mass Psychology of Ethnonationalism*. New York: Plenum Press, 1996.

Keller, T. *The Reason for God: Belief in an Age of Skepticism*. New York: Dutton, 2008.

Kimball, C. *When Religion Becomes Evil*. Harper San Francisco, 2002.

King, B. J. *Evolving God: A Provocative View on the Origins of Religion*. New York: Doubleday, 2007.

Kluger, J. "Is God in Our Genes?" *Time*, Oct. 25, 2004.

———. "What Makes Us Moral." *Time*, Dec. 3, 2007.

Koenig, H. G. *Faith and Mental Health: Religious Resources for Healing.* Philadelphia: Templeton Foundation Press, 2005.

———. *The Healing Power of Faith: Science Explores Medicine's Last Great Frontier.* New York: Simon & Schuster, 1999.

———. Cited in "Scientists Try to Study Spiritual Impact on Wellness." BeliefNet.com.

Koestler, A. *Janus: A Summing Up.* New York: Random House, 1977.

Krauss, L. "It's a Wonderful Cosmos." *New Scientist*, June 7, 2008.

Kressel, N. J. *Mass Hate: The Global Rise of Genocide and Terror.* New York: Plenum Press, 1996.

Kurtz, P. (ed). *Science and Religion: Are They Compatible?* Amherst, NY: Prometheus Books, 2003.

Lawrence, B. B. *Defenders of God: The Fundamentalist Revolt Against the Modern Age.* London: I.B. Tauris & Co. Ltd., 1990.

Lazare, D. "Among the Disbelievers." *The Nation*, May 28, 2007.

Leahy, M. P. *Letter to an Atheist.* Nashville: Harpeth River Press, 2007.

Leeming, D. *Myth: A Biography of Belief.* Oxford: Oxford University Press, 2002.

LeShan, L. *The Psychology of War: Comprehending Its Mystique and Its Madness.* New York: Helios Press, 2002.

Levin, J. *God, Faith and Health.* New York: John Wiley & Sons, 2001.

Lilla, M. *Stillborn God: Religion, Politics and the Modern West.* New York: Knopf, 2007.

———. "The Politics of God." *The New York Times Magazine*, August 19, 2007.

Lorie, P., and M. D. Mascetti. *The Quotable Spirit: A Treasury of Religious and Spiritual Quotations.* New York: Macmillan, 1996.

Luks, A., and P. Payne. *The Healing Power of Doing Good.* New York: Fawcett Columbine, 1991.

Maalouf, A. *In the Name of Identity: Violence and the Need to Belong.* New York: Arcade Publishing, 1996.

Mascall, E. L. *The Importance of Being Human: Some Aspects of the Christian Doctrine of Man.* New York: Columbia University Press, 1958.

McGrath, A. *The Dawkins Delusion: Atheist Fundamentalism and the Denial of the Divine.* London: SPCK, 2007.

————. *In the Beginning: The Story of the King James Bible*. New York: Doubleday, 2001.

McManus, S. "If God is Dead, Who Gets His House?" *The New York Times*, April 28, 2008.

McNeil, D. G. "A $10 Mosquito Net is Making Charity Cool." *The New York Times*, June 2, 2008.

Mekhennett, S., and M. Moss. "In Jihadist Haven, a Goal: To Kill and Die in Iraq." *The New York Times*, May 4, 2007.

Midgley, M. *Evolution as a Religion*. London: Routledge, 1985.

————. *Science as Salvation: A Modern Myth and Its Meaning*. London: Routledge, 1992.

Miller, K. R. *Finding Darwin's God: A Scientist's Search for Common Ground Between God and Evolution*. New York: Harper Collins, 1999.

Mitchell, S. (ed). *The Enlightened Mind: An Anthology of Sacred Prose*. Harper Collins, 1991.

Musick, M. A., J. S. House, and D. R. Williams. "Attendance at Religious Services and Mortality in a National Sample." *Journal of Health and Social Behavior*, Vol. 45, No. 2.

Nettle, D. "It Takes All Sorts." *New Scientist*, Feb. 9, 2008.

*New Scientist*. Special Report: "Beyond Belief." Jan. 28, 2006.

————. Special Report: "Fundamentalism." Oct. 8, 2005.

Niebuhr, H. R. *Faith on Earth: An Inquiry into the Structure of Human Faith*. New Haven: Yale University Press, 1989.

Nisbet, R. *History of the Idea of Progress*. New York: Basic Books, 1980.

Noble, D. F. *The Religion of Technology: The Divinity of Man and the Spirit of Invention*. New York: Alfred A. Knopf, 1997.

Novak, M. "Christopher Hitchens Is a Treasure." *National Review Online*, May 17, 2007.

————. "The Godlessness that Failed." *First Things*, June/July 2000.

————. *No One Sees God: The Dark Night of Atheists and Believers*. New York: Doubleday, 2008.

Otto, R., and B. L. Bracey. *Mysticism: East and West*. New York: Macmillan Company, 1969 (1932).

Otto, R., and J. W. Harvey (trans). *Idea of the Holy: An Inquiry into the Non-Rational Factor in the Idea of the Divine and Its Relation to the Rational*. London: Oxford University Press, 1923.

Pargament, K. I. *The Psychology of Religion and Coping*. New York: Guilford Press, 1997.

Passmore, J. *The Perfectibility of Man*. New York: Charles Scribner's Sons, 1970.

Patterson, O. "God's Gift?" *The New York Times* op-ed about spreading democracy, Dec. 19, 2006.

Payne, J. W. "A Matter of Belief or Evidence" *Washington Post Online*, June 10, 2008.

Pew Forum on Religion & Public Life, "U.S. Religious Landscape Survey," 2008.

Phillips, H. "Is God Good?" *New Scientist*, Sept. 1, 2007.

Pinker, S. "A History of Violence." Edge.org reprinted from *The New Republic*, March 19, 2007.

Post, S., and J. Neimark. *Why Good Things Happen to Good People*. New York: Broadway Books, 2007.

Putnam, R. D. *Bowling Alone: The Collapse and Revival of American Community*. New York: Simon & Schuster, 2000.

Rachels, J. *The Elements of Moral Philosophy*. New York: McGraw-Hill, 1993.

Radin, P. *Primitive Man as Philosopher*. New York: D. Appleton and Co., 1927.

———. *Primitive Religion: Its Nature and Origin*. New York: Viking Press, 1937.

Rank, O. *Art and Artist*. New York: Agathon Press, 1975 (1932).

Reat, N. R., and E. F. Perry. *A World Theology: The Central Spiritual Reality of Humankind*. Cambridge: Cambridge University Press, 1991.

Reich, W. (ed). *Origins of Terrorism: Psychologies, Ideologies, Theologies, States of Mind*. Washington, D.C.: Woodrow Wilson Center Press, 1990.

Ridley, M. *The Origins of Virtue: Human Instincts and the Evolution of Cooperation*. New York: Viking, 1997.

Royal, R. *The God that Did Not Fail: How Religion Built and Sustains the West*. New York: Encounter Books, 2006.

Ruse, M. *Darwin and Design*. Cambridge: Harvard University Press, 2003.

———. *Monad to Man: The Concept of Progress in Evolutionary Biology*. Cambridge: Harvard University Press, 1996.

Ruthven, M. *Fundamentalism: The Search for Meaning*. Oxford: Oxford University Press, 2004.

Sagan, C. *The Varieties of Scientific Experience: A Personal View of the Search for God*. New York: Penguin Press, 2006.

Sageman, M. *Leaderless Jihad*. Philadelphia: University of Pennsylvania Press, 2008.

Schacht, R. *Alienation*. New York: Doubleday & Co., 1970.

Schaefer, A. "Inside the Terrorist Mind." *Scientific American Mind*, Dec. 2007/ Jan. 2008.

Schopenhauer, A. *Religion and Other Essays*. London: Swan Sonnenschein & Co. 1893.

————. *Studies in Pessimism*. London: George Allen & Co., 1913.

Seligman, M. E. P. *Authentic Happiness*. New York: Free Press, 2002.

Shermer, M. *How We Believe: The Search for God in an Age of Science*. New York: W.H. Freeman & Co., 2000.

————. "Unweaving the Heart." *Scientific American*, October 2005.

Shweder, R. A. "Atheists Agonistes." *The New York Times* op-ed, Nov. 27, 2006.

*Skeptical Inquirer*. Special Issue: "Science, God and (Non)Belief." March/April 2007.

Skutch, A. *The Golden Core of Religion*. New York: Holt, Rinehart and Winston, 1970.

Slick, M. "Concerning Atheist Attacks on Theism" on CARM.org (Christian Apologetics & Research Ministry), 2002.

Smith, G. H. *Atheism: The Case Against God*. Amherst, NY: Prometheus Books, 1989.

Sosis, R., and E. R. Bressler. "Cooperation and Commune Longevity: A Test of the Costly Signaling Theory of Religion." *Cross-Cultural Research*, May 2003.

St. Augustine. "On the Greatness of the Soul." In Anthony Flew (ed) *Body, Mind and Death*. New York: Macmillan Co., 1964.

Stahl, W. A., R. A. Campbell, Y. Petry, and G. Diver. *Webs of Reality: Social Perspectives on Science and Religion*. New Brunswick, NJ: Rutgers University Press, 2001.

Stark, R. *For the Glory of God*. Princeton: Princeton University Press, 2003.

————. *The Victory of Reason: How Christianity Led to Freedom, Capitalism and Western Success*. New York: Random House, 2005.

Stark, R., and R. Finke. *Acts of Faith: Explaining the Human Side of Religion*. Berkeley: University of California Press, 2000.

Stark, R., and W. S. Bainbridge. *The Future of Religion*. Berkeley: University of California Press, 1985.

Stirner, M. *The Ego and His Own*. New York: Harper & Row, 1971.

Strawbridge, W. J. "Frequent Attendance at Religious Services and Mortality Over 28 Years." *American Journal of Public Health*, June 1997.

Sullivan, A., and S. Harris. "Is Religion 'Built Upon Lies?'" BeliefNet.com.

Sunstein, C. "How the Rise of the 'Daily Me' Threatens Democracy." *Financial Times* op-ed, Jan. 11, 2008.

Suzuki, D. T. *Mysticism: Christian and Buddhist*. New York: Harper & Brothers Publishers, 1957.

Szent-Gyorgyi, A. "The Drive in Living Matter to Perfect Itself." *Synthesis*, Vol. 1, No. 1, 1977.

Talmon, J. L. *Political Messianism: The Romantic Phase*. New York: Frederick A. Praeger, 1968.

Taylor, C. *A Secular Age*. Cambridge: Belknap Press of Harvard University Press, 2007.

Taylor, M. *The Fanatics: A Behavioral Approach to Political Violence*. London: Brassey's, 1991.

Taylor, M. C. "The Devoted Student." *The New York Times* op-ed, Dec. 21, 2006.

Taylor, S. E. *Positive Illusions: Creative Self-Deception and the Healthy Mind*. New York: Basic Books, 1989.

Tibi, B. *The Challenge of Fundamentalism: Political Islam and the New World Disorder*. Berkeley: University of California Press, 1998.

Tillich, P. *Dynamics of Faith: Faith and Belief: What They Are and What They Are Not*. New York: Harper & Brothers Publishers, 1957.

———. *My Search for Absolutes*. New York: Simon & Schuster, 1967.

Toch, H. *The Social Psychology of Social Movements*. New York: Bobbs-Merrill Co., 1965.

Torrence, R. M. *The Spiritual Quest: Transcendence in Myth, Religion and Science*. Berkeley: University of California Press, 1994.

Tyler, T. "The State of Trust Today." Forbes.com, Sept. 25, 2006.

University of Missouri. "Religion and Health Care Should Mix." News release, Oct. 22, 2007.

Van Biema, D. "God vs. Science." *Time*, Nov. 13, 2006.

Van Gennep, A. *The Rites of Passage*. London: Routledge & Kegan Paul, 1960 (1909).

Ward, K. *The Big Questions in Religion and Science*. West Conshohocken, PA: Templeton Foundation Press, 2008.

———. *The Case for Religion*. Oxford: One World, 2004.

———. *Is Religion Dangerous?* Grand Rapids: William B. Eerdmans Publishing Co., 2006.

Weinberg, S. *The First Three Minutes*. New York: Basic Books, 1993.

Westphal, M. *God, Guilt and Death*. Bloomington: Indiana University Press, 1984.

Wilcox, W. B. "Honoring Thy Fathers." *The Wall Street Journal*, June 13, 2008.

———. "Is Religion an Answer? Marriage, Fatherhood and the Male Problematic." Research Brief No. 11, June 2008.

Wilson, D. S. *Darwin's Cathedral: Evolution, Religion and the Nature of Society*. Chicago: University of Chicago Press, 2002.

Wilson, E. O. *Consilience: The Unity of Knowledge*. New York: Vintage Books, 1999.

———. *On Human Nature*. Cambridge: Harvard University Press, 1978.

Wilson, J. Q. *The Moral Sense*. New York: Free Press, 1993.

Wolf, G. "The Church of the Non-Believers." *Wired*, Nov. 2006.

Woodward, K. L. "Evolution as a Zero-Sum Game." *The New York Times* op-ed, Oct. 1, 2005.

Wright, R. *Non-Zero: The Logic of Human Destiny*. New York: Pantheon Books, 2000.

———. "Planet with a Purpose." BeliefNet.com.

Yardley, W. "Radical Environmentalist Gets 9-Year Term for Actions Called 'Terrorist'." *The New York Times*, May 21, 2007.

Young-Eisendrath, P., and M. E. Miller. *The Psychology of Mature Spirituality*. London: Routledge, 2000.

Zakaria, F. "Bhutto and the Future of Islam." Review of Benazir Bhutto's *Islam, Democracy and the West* in *The New York Times Book Review*, April 6, 2008.